Being and Power

A Phenomenological Ontology of Forms of Life

Daniel Rueda Garrido

Series in Philosophy

VERNON PRESS

www.vernonpress.com

In the Americas:	*In the rest of the world:*
Vernon Press	Vernon Press
1000 N West Street, Suite 1200	C/Sancti Espiritu 17,
Wilmington, Delaware, 19801	Malaga, 29006
United States	Spain

Series in Philosophy

Library of Congress Control Number: 2023950113

ISBN: 979-8-8819-0013-7

Also available: 978-1-64889-817-4 [Hardback]; 978-1-64889-855-6 [PDF, E-Book]

Cover design by Vernon Press using elements designed by Freepik.

Table of Contents

Introduction: Beings and Forms of Life

In this book, I seek to elaborate on the intuition that the understanding of what power is lies in its ontological foundation, i.e., that insofar as we are and to the degree that we are, we have power. But we are always in a particular way according to our actions and guiding principles. That is to say, we are —and are continually in— our form of life. The latter, insofar as a particular *way of being* implies a certain power to be who one wants to be, so that *a form of life is always the imposition of a particular way of being and acting —shared with a community—*. In this specific sense that I give to the term 'imposing' as that of affirming one's being through activity, the form of life that imposes itself always does so politically, that is, by affirming itself through the organisation of activity and of one's own life as a whole, taking here politics in the Aristotelian sense as that which gives *form* to life. A form of life is thus always the imposition of a particular way of acting on/by the subjects to *organize* their lives. And imposition indirectly refers to the will, which is why it is essential to understand this imposition as a free and voluntary act. In order to do so, I will discuss the relationship between being and will within the tradition from which I draw my inspiration. The task I set myself is to examine the concept of the form of life, already discussed in my previous works, in the light of its political dimension. In doing so, I seek to show that not only are power and life fused as the Spinozist-Nietzschean tradition already claimed, but that to live is always to do so by imposing a particular, non-natural or essential way of being and to expect it from or to posit it on the other individuals with whom we come into contact. The first thing I intend to do is to clarify the concept of being by looking beyond its traditional identification or vehicular relationship with language. The importance of such a task lies in showing the being that we are. A being that is but a form of life, as I claim and I hope would be clearer throughout the upcoming sections. In this last sense, this work presupposes my previous works and seeks to deepen their meaning and expand their scope. However, it is not necessary to be familiar with those works, because in this introduction I try to show their essential aspects in order to understand their connection with the theme of power and politics.

Although Fichte already used the term 'form of life' —*Lebensform*— to refer to particular realizations of the primordial life,[1] the term is nowadays mainly

---

[1] Johann Gottlieb Fichte, 'The Characteristics of the Present Age', in *Popular Works of Johann Gottlieb Fichte*, 2 vols. (London: Trübner & Co, 1889), II, p. 64. In the original, it reads: 'Die verschiedenen Gestalten in welche das Bild der Einen ewigen Urtätigkeit

associated with Ludwig Wittgenstein. For the author of the *Tractatus*, 'the world is everything that is the case'.[2] In this sense, that something is the case is a true proposition. Language seems to be the net with which we catch the world in order to know it. Because language and the world share the same logical form. That form is a shared essence. For, 'the essence of language is a picture of the essence of the world'.[3] Moreover, for Wittgenstein world and life are one.[4] Thus, what has been said so far about the world can also be applied to life. Thus, the essence of life, like the essence of the world, is expressed through language. And because essence and form are the same for Wittgenstein, life, as a form, is not a fact or an object, but 'a totality of possibilities'[5] or everything that is possible according to a form. All life is thus a form of life. Kishik's work shows that even before the *Philosophical Investigations*, Wittgenstein conceived of the concept of the form of life.[6] The question is, to what extent does the Cambridge philosopher consider the form of life or the form of the world without language, and to what extent does the form of life/the world show itself in language or does language impose its form?

On the few occasions in which Wittgenstein mentions the term form of life, a crossroads opens up, leading either to a linguistic approach centred on the uses of everyday language or to the approach to human activity. In the first case, the form of life as the ultimate foundation can only be expressed indirectly through the analysis of language games, which, in a sense, show the essence of that form of life. This is the case in which the form of life is inseparable from its linguistic expression to the point of being undifferentiated, as was the case in the *Tractatus* with language and the world. The form of life is, in this case, assimilable to language. In the second case, which is the one that interests me most, the notion of form of life is not subsumed in language, but language is subsumed in the former. Thus, language would be considered as an activity, which is

---

innerhalb unseres Bewußtseins sich bricht' [The various forms into which the image of the One eternal primordial activity is refracted within our consciousness] In *Die Grundzüge des gengenwartigen Zeltalters* (Leipzig: Verlag von Felix Meiner, 1908), Vierte Vorlesung, pp. 70-71.

[2] Ludwig Wittgenstein, *Tractatus Logico-Philosophicus* (London: Routledge and Kegan Paul Ltd, 1961), $3.01.

[3] From Wittgenstein, *Philosophical Remarks*, quoted in David Kishik, *Wittgenstein's Form of Life* (London and New York: Continuum, 2008), p. 85. Also, Wittgenstein, *Tractatus*, §2.0141.

[4] Wittgenstein, *Tractatus*, §5.621.

[5] As Kishik writes interpreting Wittgenstein's notion of life: 'As a form, life will be perceived as a totality of possibilities'. In Kishik, Wittgenstein's Form of Life, p. 12.

[6] Kiskik, *Wittgenstein's Form of Life*, pp. 25-26.

supported in a concise and isolated sentence: 'the speaking of language is part of an activity, or of a form of life'.[7]

If we take language as an activity, its meaning can no longer be established as a representation of reality or the world, as it was in the *Tractatus*. For Wittgenstein, understanding a linguistic expression seems to be the understanding of that expression in a totality that he calls a language game. This language game refers approximately —although there is no a single definition— to its relationship to other expressions and to the context in which such expressions usually appear. In other words, it requires a pragmatic knowledge of how it is used in a form of life. If we connect these elements, we can infer that the meaning of a linguistic expression is found in the form of life. In my opinion, this is the key to the bifurcation between a linguistic and an ontological interpretation of Wittgenstein's thought.

For, as I said, if the linguistic expression is understood from the form of life as a whole, the latter becomes a linguistic totality. That is, the form of life is identified with the language we use in the various language games. For 'to imagine a language means to imagine a form of life'.[8] Thus, to know the form of life is to know how we use language, to know the different language games that are given as a possibility. The form of life would be the totality of possible language games, and only of language games. This keeps us in a purely linguistic field, where life is assimilated to language. And where the language games express the essence of the former. In this way, we remain within the same limits of the *Tractatus*, by which only through language can we show or express —but not describe directly— the form of the world or the form of life, both sharing a certain logic or essence with language.[9] This is the path by which the understanding of language as activity becomes the understanding of activity as language. And the form of life thus becomes equal to that which is expressed linguistically.

On the other hand, separating ourselves from this previous path, if we emphasize the second element of the expression 'language as activity', what we obtain is one activity among others of a form of life that is not linguistic but precisely the set or totality of all the actions —and not only the language games— that are possible in it. To understand a linguistic activity or speech act —an expression forged by Austin[10] and Searle— is to understand it as an activity made possible by its form of life. The being that was assimilated to the world is now assimilated to the form of life as a totality. To understand an

---

[7] Ludwig Wittgenstein, *Philosophical Investigations* (Oxford: Blackwell, 1958), § 23.

[8] Wittgenstein, *Philosophical Investigations*, §19.

[9] Wittgenstein, *Tractatus*, § 2.18.

[10] John Austin, *How to do Things with Words* (Cambridge: Harvad University Press, 1962).

activity —even if it is a speech act— is to understand it as part of a form of life, as an actual possibility of it. It is in it that the activity obtains its own meaning. And for the same reason, to understand our activities —which implies performing them— is to understand our form of life. That form of life is the being that we are. This second path, therefore, leads us to the recognition of the form of life as a way of being and acting. In this way, by redirecting Wittgenstein's findings towards ontology, the assimilation of our being to our language is avoided. And thus, in our own actions —including our speech acts—, we can grasp who we are.

On this basis, and following the phenomenological tradition from Fichte onwards, only that which appears before our consciousness, for example our actions, can reach the status of being for us. And therefore, only that which reaches the status of being is meaningful. But, in some way, only that which we are can appear before us. That is, that which emerges from our own consciousness of what is to be human. Our self-consciousness is the consciousness of our possible actions. Consequently, that being with meaning that appears before us is our actions in the world (and that of our community). Thus, the world constituted by our possible behaviour is always pre-given in our consciousness as our horizon. In the words of Husserl: 'The world is pre-given to us [...] not occasionally but always and necessarily as the universal field of all actual and possible praxis, as horizon. To live is always to live-in-certainty-of-the-world'.[11] This ontology deals with particular beings insofar as these are forms of life, that is, a totality of meaningful actions. The abstract concept of the Being of metaphysics is reduced to the being of my form of life, which is a particular being because it is different from other forms of life. Each form of life is constituted by the subject's consciousness, as anthropical image, and the ensemble of his possible actions in the world. The latter are but constituents of the form of life, which is nothing beyond them.

As has already been made apparent, I have called 'anthropical image' to that constitutive image which structures our consciousness, and can be defined as the totality at the same time imaginary and real that we actualise with our actions in the world. Thus, the form of life is necessarily imaginary —anthropical image— and real —ensemble of actions— at the same time.[12] It must be added that the anthropical image's actualisation implies a totalising process by which the subject and the community are progressively integrated into that totality to the degree that its activity and the world in which it develops are more in line

---

[11] Edmund Husserl, *The Crisis of European Sciences and Transcendental Phenomenology* (Evanston, Illinois: Northwestern University Press, 1970), p. 142.

[12] Jean-Paul Sartre, *The Imaginary. A Phenomenological Psychology of the Imagination* (London and New York: Routledge, 2004), p. 186.

with this image of human being. Or in other words, the more I recognise myself in my actions, the more I act in the world according to the principle I identify with and vice versa; a principle that not only constitutes my consciousness but also my actions and that of my community. The latter can be defined as those subjects with whom I share my anthropical image, that is, my consciousness insofar as it is constituted by my willing that image as an inherent goal, for as Fichte lucidly says: 'the will is the proper primary root of man himself, to form the human being';[13] a will that is, after all, implied in Sartre's well-know dictum: 'In fashioning myself, I fashion man'.[14]

Albeit briefly, it is worth discussing here that precisely because of this constitutive character of the form of life, no subject can 'have' —I would rather say 'be', perhaps forcing the language— more than one form of life at the same time, but successively, after a conversion from one to another. Thus, it is not appropriate to equate the form of life with a culture or a society; if anything, it might be closer to the philosophical sense Aristotle gives it when he speaks of 'types of life', namely the life of pleasure, the life of honour, the contemplative life and the life of making money.[15] The Stagirite reduces the types of life to four of them, but I would concede that there are many more forms of life, which can be defined by the guiding principle, such as maximising economically, seeking pleasure, seeking knowledge and wisdom, living austerely, surviving, seeking alienation, maximising the glory of a god, seeking self-improvement, maximising collective benefits, etc.[16]

Now, if the essential identity of the subject is given by the image of the human being which constitutes his consciousness as the principle of his possible actions, how can he have multiple identities? This is something that does not seem paradoxical to authors such as Amartya Sen, for whom identities do not seem to be constitutive but rather external and temporary labels that one puts on and takes off; and t hus, the communities formed by them would be infinite, such as those individuals who play tennis, those who believe in aliens, those who like dogs, and so on: 'The same person can be, without any contradiction, an American citizen, of Caribbean origin, with African ancestry, a Christian, a liberal, a woman, a vegetarian, a long-distance runner, a historian, a schoolteacher, a novelist, a feminist, a heterosexual, a believer in gay and lesbian rights, a theater lover, an environmental activist, a tennis fan [...] Each

---

[13] Johann Gottlieb Fichte, *Addresses to the German Nation* (Cambridge: Cambridge University Press, 2009), p. 23.

[14] Jean-Paul Sartre, *Existentialism and Humanism* (London: Methuen, 1946), p. 30.

[15] Aristotle, *Nicomachean Ethics*, in *Complete Works*, edited by Jonathan Barnes (Princeton, Jersey: Princeton University Press, 1995), 1095 b10-1096 a10, pp. 3723-724.

[16] For the outline of several forms of life as I understand them, see my previous work.

of these collectivities, to all of which this person simultaneously belongs, gives her a particular identity'.[17] Sen takes those mentioned collectivities to be actual identities, for he continues: 'None of them can be taken to be the person's only identity or singular membership category. Given our inescapably plural identities, we have to decide on the relative importance of our different associations and affiliations in any particular context'.[18]

Now, most of the 'identities' mentioned are external labels, such as the race one belongs to or the place where someone lives; others, such as opinions on an issue or liking and disliking, do not seem sufficient to be considered identities, and in any case, my opinions and emotions depend on an identity which is the image I have of myself as a human being and which I share in an essential way with other subjects. Otherwise, the very experience of being part of a community with which one identifies oneself, or the experience of becoming progressively more integrated into it, disappears; and that implies the disappearing of a sense of belonging and self-identity as an absence of reflective consciousness about the form of life that they are effectively actualising through their behaviours. If we take as identity the different aspects of our subjectivity, what we do is to multiply unnecessarily what defines us, and we end thinking we are different because we like Netflix series, eating out and tourist travelling... when this is rather common to all subjects who share the same form of life, as 'variations of the same'.[19] The multiplication of identities can lead to taking triviality as the essence. Thus, I claim that we incarnate a single form of life successively, and that changing from one to another is a transformation or conversion preceded by a crisis as a personal —profound— experience,[20] something for which those who defend plural identities cannot account.

Having read until here, one might still wonder whether this ontology is really necessary to understand what power consists of, why this ontology or why power is rooted in being, and why power could not be conceived merely as an interpersonal relationship or a constraint of the individual at the institutional level? All these questions make sense. To answer the former, I begin by

---

[17] Amartya Sen, *Identity and Violence* (New York and London: Norton and Company, 2007), pp. xii-xiii.

[18] Amartya Sen, *Identity and Violence*, pp. xiii. Italics are mine.

[19] Byung-Chul Han, *The Disappearance of Rituals* (Cambridge: Polity Press, 2020), p. 32. My claim is also supported by this author's book titled *The Expulsion of the Other* (Cambridge: Polity Press, 2018). The following sentence comprises one of its main ideas: 'The world is peopled by clones, yet each paradoxically wants to be different from the others' (p. 11).

[20] Daniel Rueda Garrido, 'Forms of Life and The Phenomenological Ontology of Conversion', *Sophia. International Journal of Philosophy and Traditions,* 62 (2023), 33-47, https://doi.org /10.1007/s11841-021-00838-4.

addressing the latter. At the interpersonal level as at the institutional level, what we call power is exercised through an authority that is taken as given, fixed and unquestionable. The parent over the child, the teacher over the pupil, the boss over the employee, some subjects over others, the State over all its citizens, and so on. At this level, understanding can only be that of facts, which are enclosed in themselves, facts that are presented in isolation but with the guarantees of their existence as something definitively given. The ontology of forms of life is the attempt to go beyond the given, including historical and/or legislative reasons —which are no less presented as given and indisputable. Power, as interpersonal and institutional relations, relates to subjects in an equally given form of life, as its facticity; to find an understanding of power and its distribution in a form of life, one must do so from an ontology that shows the given in its ultimate grounding; power established not as something accidental that contingently curdles in its present state, but as an active structure that necessarily sustains the political and social organisation based on a particular form of life.

This ontology is necessary, in a word, to investigate power relations from the source that nourishes them: the being that subjects have endowed themselves with by adopting their form of life. In it, power is already interpersonal and hierarchical, its self-imposition is the imposition of a community and an internal hierarchy, but above all, it is the imposition of a shared identity as a particular way of being and acting, which is opposed to that of those who do not share it, the Others. Power as an external relationship with these others also has its roots in that being that we give ourselves through the form of life with which we identify. Nicolai Hartmann wrote regarding the need to make explicit the ontology in which our view is founded: 'No philosophy can stand without a fundamental view of being. This holds true regardless of standpoint, tendency, or the general picture of the world which it adopts. The reason why not every philosophy begins with a discussion of being lies in the ease with which in this field ideas are accepted and laid down undiscussed'.[21]

And yet, accepting my premises, I could still be questioned as follows: what can we learn from this ontology, and what can we do with it? Is it a kind of relativism? Are there any ethical consequences derived from the conception of being as a form of life? Beginning with the first question, what I consider of greatest significance in the conception of the form of life as an ontological unit —in-itself-for-itself— is that in it the traditional dualities of philosophy, namely, self-other, body-mind, inside-outside, being-power, are condensed in a unitary way. This unifying synthesis does not, however, as I hope to show, fuse

---

[21] Nicolai Hartmann, *New ways of Ontology* (Chicago: Henry Regnery Company, 1953), p. 4.

individual differences, differences that belong to an ontological level dependent on the universal-particular —the form of life shared by a community.

To comment briefly on how these syntheses are obtained and how they operate, I will say, first of all, that in the shared form of life, the self has an intersubjective understanding of itself as a subject that shares his way of living, so that for him to live like this, the others must also live in the same way, the exception being what we can call the absolute-Others, those who follow another form of life, and therefore are not members of the same community. The form of life, moreover, as a unity constituted by the totality of the possible actions or habits of the subject is intrinsically a union of mind-body, namely the actions that the subject grasps as necessary possibilities for himself —and his community—the action as such is an affirmation of the subject himself as a psychophysical unity. In this ontology, as we have already seen, the inner and the outer are correlative, and if the form of life is the totality of possible actions, the pre-reflective consciousness of these possibilities is what I have called the anthropical image, the image one has of oneself —and of the community— as a human being; the possibilities of acting in the world are determined by that image, which is what constitutes the subject's original self-consciousness; if the form of life is the outside or facticity, the anthropical image is the inside, but the two are but a unity, so that the one demands the other and the other the one.

Finally, by reducing the being-as-language of the metaphysics to the being-as-form-of-life —the latter in terms of principled actions in the world—, I am at the same time bringing the idea of power down from the plane of discourses and symbolic labels to the plane on which the lives of different communities unfold. I mean thus to explore power as a real manifestation of a form of life in its ontological structure. This means that power takes on different characteristics in different forms of life. If being physically stronger implies having more power than others in a form of life whose constitutive ontological principle is to survive, the powerful being those who aggressively impose themselves on others, in forms of life whose principles are maximising economic goods, expressing themselves aesthetically, pursuing wisdom or maximising the glory of God, the powerful will be respectively the one who is able to maximise the most individual benefits; the one who imposes his form of aesthetic self-expression; the one who has attained wisdom to the greatest degree; or the one who has self-imposed a life closest to that of sacrifice for the glory of God. Power in these and other cases follows the same structure but is distinguished by the form of life in which it is manifested. What I intend to show here is precisely that power is ontologically founded, and that just as one incarnates in different degrees a form of life, so on that gradual scale, power is distributed. In this way, responding once again to the relation between being and power, it can be said that if the form of life gives being to the subject, power lies precisely in self-imposing it and advancing in it, becoming what one already is and has the power to be, but this being, and its power, can only present itself as mere resistance when it is subsumed (in the process of assimilation) under a form of life that is not its own, subjected to the absolute-Other.

The latter —answering the last two questions— does not give rise to relativism in the traditional sense of the term, but neither does a universal ethical consequence follow from it, and it does nothing of the sort for the following reasons: first, the ontological constitution of each form of life certainly implies a different way of being, acting, feeling and even valuing in each form of life, and this could be understood as relativism, but what it wants to show and I think can be clearly understood from the perspective opened up by this ontology is why we cling to our way of being and doing things considering it as the best possible and superior to any other. That is, it shows why, for each subject, his or her form of life is the best possible, and does not judge whether it certainly is or not, for such a judgement is, from the outset, invalidated. On the contrary, the point is rather to explore and understand why we are not relativists in a practical sense, for we accept only our form of life. This connects with the issue of ethics; contrary to other ontologies, this ontology does not lead to universal ethics, precisely because all ethics are internal to a form of life. It is the discursive justification of a particular form of life, so that universal ethics is by definition impossible, because it can be seen, rather, how all supposedly universal ethics have been nothing but the imposition of a form of life and its ethical-justifying discourse on the other communities. For each subject and each community, its way of living and acting is the best possible by definition, otherwise, it would change through a conversion process —this is an ontological principle. Thus, there is no other ethics than that of the herd or the tribe. The only exception that can be admitted is that of the generosity of the one who opens himself to the being, doing and feeling of the other form of life at the risk of ceasing to be who he is, which is more a spontaneous and temporary attitude than the expression of an ethical system, as I also hope to show in the course of these pages.

Two Words About the Method

Finally, I would not like to end this introduction without devoting a few words to the method employed, which consists of three hierarchical but interdependent procedures. These are the following: the transcendental level, corresponding to the form of life as a transcendental structure constituted by a set of actions and guided, in turn, by an anthropical image; the empirical-perceptual level, as that in which data from the empirical sciences, such as sociology, anthropology, history and psychology, are used; and the phenomenological level, which serves as a bridge between the transcendental and the empirical. The transcendental level is the condition of possibility of the phenomenological, and this is corroborated by the empirical level. If the transcendental level is the decisive and determining one, without the data of experience and the analysis of actions in the world, that level is pure form. If the phenomenological level takes its data from consciousness —description of its intentional object— and the empirical level from the results of sensible exploration —perception and empirical data of the sciences—, the transcendental level claims the philosophical intuition of the principles revealed to consciousness and expressed in actions, i.e., the principles that in the other two levels are taken for granted. For, in philosophy as well as in science, we cannot honestly get rid of the intuition that a posteriori is validated, in some cases by arguments and empirical evidence, and in other cases by experience itself. Without intuition of the principles as the law of a given inter-subjective totality, there can be neither knowledge nor praxis.[22] Given the interdependence of the three procedures, it seems reasonable that the method of this book is to present them in parallel, reinforcing each other. The empirical data prove and shed light on the phenomenological level and the phenomenological level on the transcendental one. All three are necessary in a phenomenological ontology of the forms of life, in which our actions have to be understood in the light of our subjective experience and of the form of life as an ontological unit at the same time transcendental (anthropical image) and immanent (ensemble of actions).

Bourdieu understood the need to examine the last two levels I have referred to in an interrelated way, that is, the phenomenological and the empirical, which he calls physical. In this way, he thinks that the social sciences must rid themselves of both subjectivism and objectivism,[23] because the empirical social level determines the presuppositions of the phenomenological level, passing off as objective what is nothing but a projection onto the object —par excellence, society as an object— of the social structures that determine the subject from the outset. This is nothing more than bringing the paradox of the observer in Heisenberg's principle of indeterminacy into the realm of the social sciences. The observer, as such, is already a participant, and therefore observes

---

[22] The interdependence between intuition and observation has consistently been defended by Thomas J. Scheff, who wrote, 'as Peirce and many others have suggested, scientific inquiry is not merely inductive, but also deductive, a mixture of imagination and observation'. In *Emotions, the Social Bond and Human Reality. Part/Whole Analysis* (New York: Cambridge University Press, 1997), p. 229.

[23] Pierre Bourdieu, *The Logic of Practice* (Stanford, California: Stanford University Press, 1990), p. 52.

from certain presuppositions, which he then projects as objective and necessary. Bourdieu puts it this way. [24]

If Bourdieu believes it is necessary to take into account the phenomenological level as well as the empirical —or physical— level, and at the same time the relation of the condition of possibility of one with respect to the other, so that both subjectivism and objectivism are corrected, the matter changes when a third transcendental and immanent element is introduced on which both the experience and the —social— action performed and perceived depend. That element is the form of life, which, as transcendental, is an anthropical image that constitutes our consciousness, and, as immanent, enables and guides our actions. When Bourdieu speaks of the phenomenological level, he assumes that this is the subjective experience of performing actions whose condition of possibility is given by social structures. So, the experience I have of myself is conditioned by my status and by my social class, as if social classes were a fixed and original entity, not constituted by the objectification of the subjective experience of a community. So, if it is true that my social situation conditions me, it is no less true that this social situation is conditioned by the consciousness of individuals. But not only in the sense of endowing certain social practices with certain meanings specific to the group to which they adhere, or what Bourdieu calls *habitus*:

> The conditions associated with a particular class of conditions of existence produce *habitus*, systems of durable, transposable dispositions, structured structures predisposed to function as structuring structures, that is, as principles which generate and organize practices and representations that can be objectively adapted to their outcomes without presupposing a conscious aiming at ends or an express mastery of the operations necessary in order to attain them.[25]

Rather, this social situation is conditioned by a consciousness of what it is to be human and how to act, i.e., the subject's image of himself as a human being equally postulated in others. This third level is somehow, without being recognised by Bourdieu (who rather looks for the logic of actions in social conditions), already present in the notion of *habitus*, for there can only be a particular way of acting if it responds to a certain totality which, while not constraining unrealised possibilities, does limit the possible possibilities. This transcendental consciousness or anthropical image is also what I conceive as the condition of possibility for the actions performed by the individual to have

---

[24] Bourdieu, *The Logic of Practice*, p. 27.
[25] Bourdieu, *The Logic of Practice*, p. 53.

meaning for him; otherwise, a *habitus* that is only a social reproduction of perceived actions does not imply a true HABIT or the expression of a certain identity. Now, if we ask: where does the homogeneity of the *habitus* come from? Bourdieu answers that the *habitus* as a 'structuring structure' [26] is the principle to which individuals who share the same social and existential conditions are exposed.[27] And he gives a social class (in-itself) as 'a class of identical or similar conditions of existence and conditionings' which 'is at the same time a class of biological individuals having the same *habitus*, understood as a system of dispositions common to all products of the same conditionings'.[28] But if the habitus is acquired precisely from the external environment, i.e., the actions and objective realisations common to a group of individuals, these actions and objective realisations must be produced by this *habitus*, so that although it is contingent, once it is constituted, it is necessarily expressed in all meaningful actions of the group and excludes actions that are at odds with it:

> Being the product of a particular class of objective regularities, the *habitus* tends to generate all the 'reasonable', 'common-sense', behaviours (and only these) which are possible within the limits of these regularities, and which are likely to be positively sanctioned because they are objectively adjusted to the logic characteristic of a particular field, whose objective future they anticipate. At the same time, 'without violence, art or argument', it tends to exclude all 'extravagances' ('not for the likes of us'), that is, all the behaviours that would be negatively sanctioned because they are incompatible with the objective conditions.[29]

This exclusion of actions considered extravagant has its motivation in the *habitus* —or principle— rather than in the objective conditions of existence, as Bourdieu wants, because those conditions, which are the behaviours of individuals with respect to other individuals and with respect to things, are originally based on that *habitus* —or principle. The *habitus*, as an enabling, emergent and contingent structure, organises actions and marks them with its 'modus operandi'.[30] Therefore, in order for the *habitus* to have a unity recognised by both the one who perceives these actions and the one who produces them,[31] it must have a certain transcendence so that the principle that guides an action is not only proper to that action but is also understood to guide others equally

---

[26] Bourdieu, *The Logic of Practice*, p. 53.
[27] Bourdieu, *The Logic of Practice*, p. 59.
[28] Bourdieu, *The Logic of Practice*, p. 59.
[29] Bourdieu, *The Logic of Practice*, pp. 55-56.
[30] Bourdieu, *The Logic of Practice*, p. 57.
[31] Bourdieu, *The Logic of Practice*, p. 58.

marked by the same identity. The homogeneity of behaviours to which the *habitus* gives rise requires a transcendental consciousness of which the *habitus* is the principle, namely, a pre-reflective image of being human. It is this transcendental consciousness that gives unity, immediate non-reflective meaning, and homogeneity to behaviours. This also explains why when there is a change in social conditions, the group or community persists in its *habitus*, which is not easily explained if one considers that social conditions produce the habitus without any filtering by the consciousness and identification of the subjects. Bourdieu acknowledged this persistence of the *habitus* over the changes in social conditions: 'The tendency of groups to persist in their ways, due *inter alia* to the fact that they are composed of *individuals with durable dispositions that can outlive the economic and social conditions* in which they were produced, can be the source of misadaptation as well as adaptation, revolt as well as resignation'.[32] Why, then, do the new social conditions not produce a new habitus? I suggest that the answer lies in the constitutive self-image as a human being or anthropical image that the community shares and expresses in its actions.

To say that the structure is already in every action is equally correct, I do not deny it; on the contrary, it is fundamental to affirm it because the group or community is recognised precisely by that structure, principle or *habitus* which guides and constitutes their actions, which reaffirms them as members of the group and constitutes 'their world'. But for this principle or *habitus* to guide behaviour and mark it with its 'modus operandi' requires a self-consciousness as a human being who behaves in this particular way, even if this self-consciousness is not necessarily reflective. This is because, as Bourdieu well understands, the *habitus* or principle does not give rise to automatic behaviour,[33] but to behaviours that are meaningful to the agents who carry them out. Even if, as I say, they are not reflectively aware of that principle, they are aware that they are performing an action that is meaningful to them. And by the same token, this ensures that the actions of others who share that principle or *habitus* are immediately, or unreflectively, understood as meaningful, and that even those imitated actions would not be imitated if there were no identification of the subject with their 'modus operandi'. Bourdieu recognises that when our body adopts the same movements that we are perceiving in another, we unreflectively imitate an other with whom, nevertheless, a certain identification is required.[34]

---

[32] Bourdieu, *The Logic of Practice*, p. 62.

[33] 'Through the *habitus*, the structure of which it is the product governs practice, *not along the paths of a mechanical determinism but within the constraints and limits initially set on its inventions*'. In Bourdieu, *The Logic of Practice*, p. 55. Italics are mine.

[34] Bourdieu, *The Logic of Practice*, p. 73.

And he goes on to add that when there is no explicit education or the pedagogical action is diffuse, 'the essential part of the modus operandi that defines practical is transmitted through practice, in the practical state, without rising to the level of discourse. The child mimics other people's actions rather than "models"'.[35] That modus operandi that is transmitted, as stated in the second quote, requires the identification discussed in the first quote. As Zahavi has shown and I have discussed elsewhere,[36] there is no imitation without the pre-reflective self-consciousness that enables our identification with the other subject.[37]

By this I do not mean to undervalue Bourdieu's intellectual work or his findings, especially that of *habitus*, but to point out that what the French sociologist did not contemplate is that this notion of *habitus* presupposes a unitary transcendental consciousness by which the latter is constituted as a true mental and behavioural habit and not just a series of actions repeated by an automaton, alienated as a subject. A *habitus*, in order to become such, and, therefore, to constitute all our actions and attitudes, must be more than a mere acquired routine that does not modify consciousness. It has to be the principle of the subjectivity of the individual and his community. That is, a principle that gives unity and meaning to our actions precisely because it expresses our original self-consciousness or image of ourselves as human beings. In our actions, we therefore recognise ourselves or not, depending on whether the principle that directs them expresses this anthropical image. On the contrary, to presuppose that it is social and existential conditions that dictate our *habitus* is to fail to recognise that in them, there is already an invested consciousness, as one that acts in a world that it transforms through its actions. The essence of my approach lies in this, showing what is necessarily presupposed.

---

[35] Bourdieu, *The Logic of Practice*, pp. 73-74.

[36] Daniel Rueda Garrido, *Forms of Life and Subjectivity. Rethinking Sartre's Philosophy* (Cambridge: Open Book Publishers, 2021), pp. 123-146; Dan Zahavi, 'Empathy and Mirroring: Husserl and Gallese', in *Life, Subjectivity & Art: Essays in Honor of Rudolf Bernet*, ed. by Roland Breeur and Ullrich Melle (Dordrecht: Springer, 2012), pp. 217–54.

[37] The same has been underlined by Jean-Luc Nancy, who uses the terms *mimesis* and *methexis* for what I have been calling 'imitation' and 'identification' respectively. He wrote: 'No *mimesis* occurs without *methexis* —or else be merely copy, reproduction— that is the principle. Reciprocally, no doubt, no *methexis* without implicating *mimesis*', Jean-Luc Nancy, 'The Image: mimesis and methexis', *Nancy and Visual Culture*, ed. by Adrienne Janus and Carrie Giunta (Edinburgh: Edinburgh University Press, 2016), pp. 73-92 (p. 75). Nancy describes methexis as participation in something that is imitated by taking it as a model.

Outline of Contents

Having defined the main concepts, the method and the philosophical position from which I start, the investigation to which I devote this book is to explore how the being that we are as a form of life has its source in the will, which implies a certain power. To this end, I begin the first chapter with a review of four philosophies of the will. I reject the identification between instinct and will supported by Nietzsche and Schopenhauer, and weigh the identification between will and consciousness as considered by Sartre and Fichte. I claim a notion of WILL as self-affirmation of the subject through all meaningful action. I argue that the will is not just consciousness, but conscious activity expressed through actions in the world. This affirmation of oneself (and one's community) is the will-to-be, while both the act of self-affirmation and the expansion derived from the imposition on other individuals and communities is the exercise of the will-to-power. Both wills are dimensions of the same WILL, which is realised as the imposition of a form of life to the exclusion of others. This will is thus political, since, in discussion with Aristotle, I argue that the political is the constitution and organisation of life according to a single image of what is to be human.

In chapter two, I analyse how, at the phenomenological level, the affirmation of the self through the affirmation of the form of life is driven by self-interest, which is how the dimension of power is translated —in parallel with that of being. I show that our interest depends on our image of being human and that the realisation of this is our primary interest, as well as the affirmation of our disinterest in all that denies or threatens our being. Our interest in being runs parallel to our disinterest in that way of being which undermines our interest, for the latter has repercussions on our own subjectivity and identity. Here, I discuss in dialogue with Ricoeur how the subject that affirms himself by pursuing his interest constitutes an identity that is maintained over time — identity as selfhood— and that is also identity by comparison with other subjects —identity as sameness. Thanks to the former, we recognise ourselves in our actions, and, thanks to the latter, we recognise our co-subjects and together as members of a shared community.

In chapter three, I set out in detail the relationship between the will-to-power and the universalisation of the form of life. The will-to-power, as defined in the first chapter, is the dimension of the will that imposes the self on the subject himself or on other individuals and other forms of life. If we have called the former 'self-affirmation' in one's own way of being and acting, we call the latter 'universalisation' of that way of being and acting. I discuss this concept with Žižek, Butler and Laclau. And I conclude that if, as these authors argue, the universal cannot be universal without the particular, hegemony is achieved when this universal-particular, or the universal of a community, is universalised.

I therefore distinguish between universal, universalisation and universal-particular. This universalisation is resisted by what Sloterdijk calls the resistance of the 'kynical' as the one that will only follow a way of being and acting with which he identifies himself; a resistance that I argue is inseparable from the structural tendency to assimilation in all forms of life.

Having dealt with the aspects of the affirmation and universalisation of being, in chapter four, I deal with the third aspect of the will, namely the spontaneity of the process. This aspect is the will-to-will, which, in dialogue with Fichte, Heidegger and Deleuze, I associate with life or existence, emphasising its indissolubility with the form of life. Existence, as the will-to-will, is the driving force of the form of life, but it is not prior to it, but simultaneous and immanent. For the will-to-will on the transcendental level is constitutive of the will-to-be, even if, phenomenologically, the latter has its possibility in the constitutive opposite that it posits as its negation. Ultimately, the possibility of being is in the will-to-be, which has to deny itself in its will-to-will aspect, without ceasing to be constituted by it.

In the last chapter, I examine the importance of the limits of power, both for its own constitution and for its overcoming. For the power that eliminates its limits eliminates itself. The limits I identify are life (its constitutive opposite) and the Other (which resists). Both the elimination of life, with its associated generosity, through the progressive grounding of being as a form of life, and the elimination of the Other, as everything that submits to a different form of life, leads to self-destruction. If the suspension of being brings us closer to that impossible experience of life that constitutes us as a possibility of possibilities and a will-to-will, I argue that this suspension is the temporary rupture of the political —conceived as a form of life— and the opposite of power. This suspension has a mystical root, sustained in the absence of being and acting.

At the conclusion of the book, the issues addressed in the various chapters are not only presented synthetically and coherently, but I try to make more sense of them by discussing how the form of life is at the ontological origins of State formation without the State being strictly necessary for the form of life as such. The constitution of the State through the institutionalisation of a form of life by government over a society or group of individuals results in its legitimation or lack thereof depending on whether or not those individuals identify with the institutionalised form of life. I discuss the relationship between community, social group and State, as well as the various ways in which the State marginalises and rejects minorities, understood as communities that share a form of life different from the hegemonic or institutionalised one in a given national territory. I seek to establish solutions to the problem of State conflict as an extension of the conflict between communities that incarnate different forms of life. Power, once again, has to confront generosity, for there is no possible ethics that can avoid conflict, since all ethics is that of one form of life and seeks to affirm and advance it against Others. In any case, ethics can only prevent the assimilation of some States by Others, justifying resistance against the power that seeks its universalisation. As throughout the book, generosity remains the only final solution, a subversive generosity, to which philosophy exposes us, which is thus situated as a dangerous activity, for the generosity that comes from the doubt and questioning that the philosopher directs towards himself is an explosive in the foundations of the form of life as will-to-power and, therefore, of the State in which it has been institutionalised. Generosity is the suspension of being and thus the absence of power and the universalisation of one's own being: it is letting Others be by revealing the constitutive and inevitable ontological predicament, and thus the absurdity of the will-to-be.

Chapter 1

Philosophies of the Will

The question that will guide the following sections is what it is that makes a form of life persist in its being, for what is may well not be. So, we thus confront the Heideggerian question of 'why are there beings instead of nothing', now modified: 'why are there forms of life instead of absurd and impenetrable mere existence? As in Spinoza's case, the answer is to be found in the concept of *conatus*, namely, the will-to-be (or *voluntas* and *cupiditas*), for according to him, 'to be able to exist is power';[1] hence, it is now necessary to analyse the form of life in its constitutive dimension as power. The form of life is power insofar as it perseveres in its being. And that is why, on another level of analysis, culture is also power. And, on the contrary, *a form of negativity* is the absence of power and the one that experiences the domination of the form of life. We must bear in mind that a form of life is power because it is a will-to-be. The will-to-be is the will to affirm itself as a form of life, but the form of life is the self-imposition of a universal, because the principle that drives it is the will to realise its anthropical image in the world. Consequently, the self-affirmation of the form of life is also universalisation and expansion. The universalisation of one form of life means the negation and assimilation of other forms of life. Thus, the form of life is driven by the will-to-power insofar as it is a will-to-be (to be more intensely and perfectly who one already is in the original self-consciousness) through its constituents —principle and actions.

From this, it follows that our will-to-power is nothing more than our will-to-be from the aspect of its imposition both on oneself, which we call self-affirmation, and on others, which we will treat as universalisation. Both are, however, tendencies of one and the same will. For being is a matter of wanting to be and, above all, of maintaining or persisting in that being. This would be a difference with respect to animals, who cannot decide what they want to be; they merely live, willing through their existence to keep willing. The human being, in what has been taken as his 'unfinished character' not only can but must decide who he wants to be. In this sense, Max Scheler sees human beings to be essentially open to constituting their own world: 'Human beings can not only elevate the "environment" to the dimension of "world" and turn "resistances" into "objects", but they can also -and this is the most admirable

---

[1] Benedictus Spinoza, *Ethics*, in *Complete Works* (Indianapolis, Cambridge: Hackett Publishing Company, 2002), part 1, Prop. 11, p. 222.

thing- make their own physiological and psychological constitution and each of their mental experiences objective. This is precisely why they can also freely shape their own life'.[2] It is what Sartre —but also Fichte— expressed with his well-known motto, 'man [we all] are condemned to be free'.[3] And the same can be said from a genetic point of view with respect to the community of subjects; the latter is the actualisation of a particular will-to-be expressed through their behaviour, which becomes facticity, that is, in Scheler's terms, objective experiences.

1.1. Four Philosophies of the Will

This wanting has been conceived as instinct by some, such as Nietzsche and Schopenhauer, and therefore something biological or physiological, determined by our nature, which thus tries to persevere as a species, for if we did not desire 'by ascetic renunciation of pleasure and refusal of what is necessary to sustain existence', we would cease to live.[4] With our desires we make concrete the universal energy of nature or *desiring desire* that pushes us to keep living, as blind will-to-live —in an anticipation of Darwin's ideas of survival of the fittest:[5] 'it is not the individual that nature cares for, but only the species; and in all seriousness she urges the preservation of the species, since she provides for this so lavishly through the immense surplus of the seed and the great strength of the fructifying impulse';[6] a concrete but illusory life 'that deceive[s] those who see the world through the veil of Maya', [7] for it is nothing more than the way in which nature perseveres as the vital energy of the universe, by means of the

---

[2] 'Kraft seines Geistes vermag das Wesen, das wir "Mensch" nennen, nicht nur die Umwelt in die Dimension des Weltseins zu erweitern und Widerstände gegenständlich zu machen, sondern es vermag auch —und das ist das Merkwürdigste— seine eigene physiologische und psychische Beschaffenheit und jedes einzelne psychische Erlebnis, jede einzelne seiner vitalen Funktionen selbst wieder gegenständllich zu machen. Nur darum vermag dieses Wesen auch sein Leben frei von sich zu werfen'. In Max Scheler, *Die Stellung des Menschen in Kosmos* (Bonn: Bouvier Verlag, 1991), pp. 41-42. Translation is mine.

[3] Jean-Paul Sartre, *Existentialism and humanism* (London : Methuen, 1960), p. 34; in Sartre, *L'existentialism est un humanisme* (Paris: Les Éditions Nagel, 1966), p. 37 : 'l'homme est condamné à être libre'.

[4] Jenny Bunker, 'Ethics and Will in Schopenhauer's Philosophy', in *The Concept of Will in Classical German Philosophy*, ed. by Manja Kisner and Jörg Noller (Berlin and Boston: De Gruyter, 2020), pp. 147-162 (p. 254).

[5] Charles Darwin, *The Origin of Species by Means of Natural Selection* (Cambridge: Cambridge University Press, 2009).

[6] Arthur Schopenhauer, *The World as Will and Representation*, 2 vols (New York: Dover Publications, Inc., 1969), I., p. 276.

[7] Jenny Bunker, 'Ethics and Will in Schopenhauer's Philosophy', in *The Concept of Will in Classical German Philosophy*, ed. by Manja Kisner and Jörg Noller (Berlin and Boston: De Gruyter, 2020), pp. 147-162 (p. 251).

deception that Schopenhauer calls *principium individuationis* —the liberation of desire, with its consequent suffering, being the reintegration into the primordial vital unity: 'It is true that we see the individual come into being and pass away; but the individual is only phenomenon, exists only for knowledge involved in the principle of sufficient reason, in the *principium individuationis*'.[8] In a certain way, and contrary to his teacher, in Nietzsche, it is the will-to-power or the will to affirm one's own life by means of his desires and instincts what is promoted.[9] But, in both, it is those instincts in which the will-to-live is fathomed that determine our representations or interpretations of the world; in Schopenhauer's words: 'Through the addition of the world as representation, developed for its service, the will obtains knowledge of its own willing and what it wills, namely that this is nothing but this world, life, precisely as it exists. We have therefore called the phenomenal world the mirror, the objectivity, of the will'.[10] And in Nietzsche, we find something similar: 'Our empirical world would be determined by the instincts of self-preservation even as regards the limits of its knowledge: we would regard as true, good, valuable that which serves the preservation of the specie'.[11]

Others, however, have seen in the will a drive closely related to or identical to the intellect, such as Spinoza, Fichte,[12] Schelling, and, to a certain extent, also Sartre. With the latter, one could say that the will is the spontaneity of consciousness in its intentional relation to the world, or, in other words, the capacity of consciousness to freely present its objects. The will of the human being would be a dimension of consciousness in as much as its essence is freedom: 'the will is not a privileged manifestation of freedom but that it is a psychic event of a peculiar structure which is constituted on the same plane as other psychic events and which is supported, neither more nor less than the others, by an original, ontological freedom'.[13] The will-to-be this or that type of

---

[8] Schopenhauer, *The World as Will and Representation*, I., p. 275.

[9] Contrary to Schopenhauer's ethics of compassion, 'Seneca, Aristotle, Spinoza, Mill and Nietzsche held self-interest to be in harmony with morality (...) Schopenhauer gives us no convincing reason to accept his picture of moral value as exhausted by compassion and antithetical to egoism'. In Bunker, 'Ethics and Will in Schopenhauer's Philosophy', p. 253.

[10] Schopenhauer, *The World as Will and Representation*, I., p. 275.

[11] Nietzsche, *The Will to Power* (New York: Vintage Books, 1967), p. 313.

[12] In his article 'The Other and the Necessary Conditions of the Self in Fichte's *Wissenschaftslehre* and Paul Ricoeur's Phenomenology of the Will', Arnold L. Farr says about Fichte's unitary conception of willing and thinking: 'In the *Wissenschaftslehre* thinking and willing are coterminous. The absolute unity of thinking and willing is the original duplicity of the I'. In *Fichte and the Phenomenological Tradition*, ed. by Violetta Waibe Daniel Breazeale and Tom Rockmore (Berlin: De Gruyter, 2010), pp. 341-56 (p. 342).

[13] Jean-Paul Sartre, *Being and Nothingness* (New York: Philosophical Library, 1956), p. 452.

person (as an end or project) is spontaneous but depends on the content consciousness grasps from the world because, essentially, it is the latter in its phenomenological condensation that constitutes the consciousness of the subject as a changing whole in terms of fundamental project; the latter is the cause as grasped by the pre-reflective consciousness that becomes the motive of the will or the reflective consciousness of a particular end. As Sartre puts it, the for-itself, as a pure project towards an end, 'causes there to be a certain objective structure of the world, one which deserves the name of cause in the light of this end. The for-itself is therefore the consciousness of this cause. But this positional consciousness of the cause is on principle a non-thetic consciousness of itself as a project toward an end. In this sense it is a motive'.[14] Thus, the will, as reflective consciousness of a spontaneously self-given project, is contingent and free because it is not determined by the world but neither by human nature and its instincts, which Sartre denies: 'freedom is nothing but the existence of our will or of our passions in so far as this existence is the nihilation of facticity; that is, the existence of a being which is its being in the mode of having to be it'.[15]

At the other extreme would be Fichte, for whom the will is essentially an eternal energy, which he calls 'pure will', and which is not only the condition of possibility of our empirical will, but which determines moral life, depending on whether the empirical will submits to it or withdraws from it.[16] This pure will is related in Fichte to the drive or tendency to I's self-activity for 'the being of the I is absolute activity and nothing but activity; but activity, taken objectively, is drive';[17] and in its turn, drive is related to human instincts (*Naturtrieb*): 'I myself am, in a certain respect, nature, notwithstanding the absolute character of my reason and my freedom; and this nature of mine is a drive'.[18] However, the pure will is more than that, for it is eternal, thus the drive's position as an intermediary between nature and freedom, as Manja Kisner put it: 'With the help of the drive, we can explain rational beings as a part of nature —they are embodied in a natural organic body— but at the same time as free in their

---

[14] Sartre, *Being and Nothingness*, p. 449.

[15] Sartre, *Being and Nothingness*, p. 444.

[16] Manja Kisner, 'Drive and Will in Fichte's *System of Ethics*', in *The Concept of Will in Classical German Philosophy*, ed. by Manja Kisner and Jörg Noller (Berlin and Boston: De Gruyter, 2020), pp. 141-57.

[17] Johann Gottlieb Fichte, *The System of Ethics. According to the Principles of the Wissenschaftslehre*, ed. by Daniel Breazeale (Cambridge: Cambridge University Press, 2005), p. 101. *Gesamtausgabe*, volume 5, p. 105.

[18] Fichte, *The System of Ethics. According to the Principles of the Wissenschaftslehre*, ed. by Daniel Breazeale (Cambridge: Cambridge University Press, 2005), p. 105. *Gesamtausgabe*, volume 5, p. 108.

striving to overcome nature. In this way the concept of drive unifies both aspects —activity and cognition— and mediates between nature and freedom, respectively'.[19] Pure will is a universal energy which all beings share, and by which all are what they are, but which in the human being in a particular way is understood as the responsibility of being that which the pure will commands by means of the freely aligned will of the subject. Breazeale explains it as follows:

> [Fichte] insists on connecting the self-determination of the concretely free moral agent with that mysterious act of determination by means of which the pure will determines the original character of finite individuals, who are then able to become aware of themselves not only as this or that individual, but also –and more truly– as the pure will itself, which is something I grasp only insofar as I conceive of myself as an instrument or tool of the moral law.[20]

This pure will is, in short, an ideal of humanity that every subject would share and to which they must aspire: 'This determinacy, which constitutes my basic character, consists in the fact that I am determined to determine myself in a certain way [...] Man's determinate nature or "vocation" is not something he gives to himself; instead, it is that through which a human being is a human being'.[21] Thus, if, in Sartre, the will is contingent and spontaneous as a dimension of consciousness and only takes its content from the world; the will in Fichte would be derived from the pure will that throbs in the empirical will and with which the latter must coincide in its essential contents to realise its essence. If both Nietzsche and Schopenhauer take the will as universal energy comprised as instincts in human beings -instincts that direct our perception and representation of the world-, on the contrary, Fichte and Sartre conceive of the human will as pure freedom over and above instincts, and in the specific case of Fichte, freedom as moral responsibility with respect to the pure will expressed in the idea of humanity. The pure will, fathomed as drive, is redirected according to the understanding of the subjects to one or another empirical will of which he is responsible, for Fichte says, 'the drive notwithstanding, I am able to determine myself in a manner contrary to the drive, just as I can also determine myself in a manner that conforms to the

---

[19] Manja Kisner, 'Drive and Will' in *Fichte's System of Ethics*, p. 152.

[20] Daniel Breazeale, 'How to Make an Existentialist? In Search of a Shortcut from Fichte to Sartre', p. 308.

[21] Johann Gottlieb Fichte, *Foundations of Transcendental Philosophy. Wissenschaftlehre Nova Methodo (1796/1799)*, ed. By Daniel Breazeale (Ithaca and London: Cornell University Press, 1992), p. 300.

drive'.[22] In this outline of the conceptions of the will of these different thinkers, various options are revealed when it comes to thinking about what the will is. And, of course, the debate about will and consciousness continues today, especially about free will. A critical examination of some of the contemporary authors on this topic has already been made elsewhere. The question is now to think for ourselves. And, in particular, to work with these ideas to express what I mean by will in this ontology of forms of life.

As has been seen, I proceed from the intuition and experience that the form of life with which we identify ourselves is what constitutes us as subjects. We are in our subjectivity those habits and regular actions of our community as well as the image it shares of what it is to be human. This 'we' is, therefore, unitary, for it contains in its unity both the driving principle and the actions. From this main intuition, we have to derive what the will is and put it in dialogue with the above-mentioned conceptions. In this sense, for the time being, I try to think between two margins: that of the reduction or parenthesis of our facticity and that of transcendental consciousness, i.e., it is a question in principle of accounting for what the will is from the phenomenological experience we have of the form of life independently of the transcendental image of being human and of the actual actions that I and my community carry out in the midst of the world. And this without discounting at any moment the imperative need of both levels, because it would not be possible to have such an experience at the phenomenological level without my anthropical image and without my community and the actions to which I am or have been exposed in some way and which I myself carry out. And why? Simply because it is at that intermediate level, that of reflection, where the two coincide and where both can be revealed in their essence and principle. That is, although I concentrate on one of the levels, the other two are at all times omnipresent and necessary as forming an inviolable unity.

1.2. The Phenomenology of the Will

To begin with, what we call 'will' cannot but be something that refers to the subject, nothing outside him or transcendent to him, not in his community nor in his pre-reflective consciousness. If it is to him that it refers, in what way does it refer to him? As something he suffers, something he causes or something he is? If it were as something he suffers, he would apprehend it as an affection or passion, that is, as being affected by it, as if his will were imposed on him without him taking part in it, something like when an arm has gone dead, and yet we manage to move it slightly, the movement and the arm do not seem to

---

[22] Fichte, *The System of Ethics*, p. 104. *Gesamtausgabe*, volume 5, p. 107.

be ours. As with the example of the arm going dead, the will can only occasionally present itself to us as expropriated, as if we were experiencing it from outside. The subject's experience is that he is the one who wills or decides his actions, and not that someone else decides for him. That this is not the case, however, may be due to varying degrees of external imposition or constraint, as well as some assimilation. That is, as with the arm that is gone dead, the will that is experienced as a passion is a weakened will that cannot firmly will what it wills and cannot firmly reject what it does not will (what usually is called 'akrasia'). This can be referred to as constriction, because the unwilling subject cannot will firmly enough to overcome the constriction and assimilation of the outside, of whoever is imposing his will upon him.

Thus, while the will can be accounted for as a passion, it does not seem proper for the will to be experienced as such by the subject except in a situation of constriction or assimilation, whereby literally the will of others is imposed by weakening the subject's identification with his own will, which is now assimilated to that of the other. That is, when we do not do what we want, but it seems to us that we do. This happens when, for example, the subject reproduces the actions of others with which he does not identify, but does so either by *constriction*, as when a heavy smoker is forbidden to smoke, —he does not put out his cigarette voluntarily, does he? In any case, is both a passive will or the reciprocity of the involuntary and voluntary, as Ricoeur put it[23]— or by *conditioning*, as when the subject in a meeting with non-smokers decides not to light up a cigarette, or by *indetermination*—i.e., indecision—, when handed his first cigarette, and without knowing how to proceed, the subject reproduces the gestures and organic functions of a friend or companion, in any case a somewhat more experienced smoker.

The involuntary aspect has to do with the conditioning of our behaviour, without this ceasing to be voluntary, since it is the subject who, in the end, carries it out, and this could not be the case given the contrary motivation. In any case, the subject has the experience of a will which, without ceasing to be his own, acts according to the conditioning received, what Ricoeur calls a 'dependent independence'.[24] To the highest degree, this conditioning is an external constraint by which the subject truly feels his will alienated. And yet all these cases presuppose the general state whereby the subject experiences that his will is not a passion but an active power; that he is the one who acts as he wills, even if, in doing that, he is conditioned. For Ricoeur, this contradictory

---

[23] Paul Ricoeur, *Freedom and Nature: The Voluntary and the Involuntary* (Evanston, Illinois: Northwestern University Press, 1966).
[24] Ricoeur, *Freedom and Nature: The Voluntary and the Involuntary*, p. 483.

union is the key to the will, and that is why he wrote: 'daring and patience never cease to alternate in the very heart of willing'.[25]

So, if the will is not phenomenologically experienced as an imposition that the subject bears, unless the subject's will is weakened, then we could say that the will refers to something that the subject causes. If this characterisation is correct, we would be talking about a will experienced as causality with respect to the world. The subject is in the power of his will, which would be a kind of instrument with which various effects are caused, transforming his environment and creating new situations. The will thus understood, is an instrument that presupposes an understanding of the end or aim of willing; a cognition, if you will. It influences the world with its will in a particular respect. The subject experiences himself as above or prior to and independent of his will, he is the one who decides, he is the one who directs his will towards the world. This is the way of conceiving will in most languages, it is a grammatical way: 'I will'. The subject that wills is ontologically and logically prior to the will. Thus, willing is an instrumental appendix of the subject ('I'). Ricoeur questions this conception on the need to know the 'who' of any activity, including willing, by which the 'who' is separated from the 'what' as a substratum: 'The person, as a referential term, remains one of the "things" about which we speak. In this sense the theory of basic particulars finally remains captive to an ontology of "something in general" which, faced with the demand for recognition of the ipse'.[26] For that conception, willing presupposes a prior identity, an 'I', which could be understood as the grammatical subject of a narrative succession, that is: 'I am the one who wills this and that, who does this and that, who says this and that...' which, in turns, it is taken to lead to the constitution of self-identity; and yet, if we pay attention and reflect critically, we might ask: do we experience ourselves as something other than our will? Or is it just a grammatical way of understanding ourselves post factum, an effect of language in our narration after our phenomenological experience of willing something? Do we experience willing as an instrument? That is to say, when the subject desires something, he distinguishes the desired thing from himself, but does it also distinguish the will from a supposedly independent identity?

If this were so, not only would we separate the subject from his will and both from the thing ('I-will-this'), which is a grammatical projection, but we also seem to be severely splitting both the subject and his being-in-the-world. For, if the subject can be distinguished from his will, it means that the will is independent, or at least accidental, not essential to the understanding of the

---

[25] Ricoeur, *Freedom and Nature: The Voluntary and the Involuntary*, p. 484.
[26] Paul Ricoeur, *Oneself as Another* (Chicago and London: Chicago University Press, 1992), p. 96.

subject in his identity. The latter could completely cease to will or desire, could know himself above and independently of his will... And yet, what is the subject without will? Can he live without addressing himself to the world, without thinking, doing, perceiving...? And isn't all this activity voluntary? Is it not the subject that voluntarily thinks, does, perceives, values, feels...? To take the will as an instrument is to reify it, to make it a thing with which to operate in the world, a means to an end. And for the same reason, the subject without will (the latter as a mere accident) is also a thing, a substance, disconnected from the world. When the subject wills rather it is he who addresses himself to the world, willing it in its totality, for when the subject thinks about or acts in the world, he does not apprehend himself as distinct from his will; he is his will reaching out to the world, presenting the world to himself through his praxical images (which I remind the reader it is an action construed as intentional object of our will/consciousness). Thus, a thing is presented as food that one wants to eat, another thing as a face that one wants to contemplate, and yet another as a physical exercise that one wants to perform, a piece of metal that one wants to grab, a book one wants to read... They are all 'recipients' of actions grasped as praxical images. The subject is all these voluntary activities, which can, however, be affected by external coercion or conditioning that weakens[27] the will and degrades the subject who wants to perform them.

If it is neither a mere passion nor an instrument, the will, by elimination, has been shown to have to do with the being of the subject himself. We are our will. There is no difference between the one who is and the one who wills, I am the one who wills, true, but I also will the one who I am. As will and being are identified, we can neither be before willing nor will before being. The will-to-be is simultaneous to being *as a possibility*. Now, how does this advance our investigation on the will? We have shown that the subject is not distinct from his will and that he posits himself in each of his desires. He cannot desire a thing without this desire constituting him in his identity, and that, therefore, his desires presuppose the will-to-be what he is. When the subject desires a thing, in this intentional relation is engraved his will to be someone who desires this type of things.[28] That is why we define ourselves with our likings and desires, in

---

[27] I leave aside for now how conditioning, when it is of the same sign as the will (i.e., they share the driving principle), tends to strengthen the latter as an occasion for the affirmation of the subject's identity. I have elaborated on this topic in various writings, see Daniel Rueda Garrido, 'Imitation, Conscious Will and Social Conditioning', *Mind and Society*, 20 (2021), 85-102; *Forms of Life and Subjectivity* (Cambridge: Open Book Publishers, 2021), and *Forms of Life: Propaganda and Ideology* (Cambridge: Ethics Press, 2023).

[28] As I say below, the intentional schema in relation to a form of life I maintain is that of a praxical image in which an action is posited in relation to a subject or a thing (non-subjects are considered things in themselves) which I call the 'recipient' of the action.

them is revealed our will-to-be a particular being. But this particular being is not exclusively individual. It cannot be if, as has been said, the subject has the will to be someone who desires certain types of things. For the coincidence in these desires is a coincidence in the will-to-be a type of human being according to his likings, desires, actions and so on. In a word, the will-to-be is the will to incarnate a certain form of life in which such actions are necessary possibilities.

Thus, when the subject is presented with a thing in the mode of desire, he acts in order to obtain it —making the thing the recipient of this action within his praxical image—, and it is, in fact, in this necessary action that will and desire are determined. But this action in intentional relation to the thing is mediated by the form of life of his community. His will to act in this way presupposes the will-to-be a member of the community, identified with its image of being human. But that is the transcendental level of which the subject is not reflectively aware. The subject of these experiences lives them as rooted in his individual being, but at all times does, thinks and feels what the human being he has as a model would do, think and feel; a model that is also shared with other subjects. In this sense, what is desired is what is necessary to be desired. He sets before himself, desiring what he understands that brings him closer to who he grasps to be -in a pre-reflective way-. Acting voluntarily he realises in the world that anthropical image with which he identifies. He feels progressively more perfect, and this perfection implies a greater reflective consciousness of the universal human image that he incarnates.

1.3. Reassessing the Philosophies of the Will

Now that our analysis has led us to the form of life, we can from it concretise our examination of the will in dialogue with the thinkers mentioned above. The will at the phenomenological level constantly requires the other ontological levels. It is the form of life as a unity where being and will coincide. In the subject, this coincidence derives from being an incarnation of the form of life. This, as already said, is *in-itself-for-itself*. This is consciousness or driving principle and action in the world. The subject is the consciousness of the actions that are proper to the human being with which he identifies himself, a human being enacted by his community. Consciousness is the condition of possibility of such actions, which are necessary in their possibility —while rejecting those grasped as impossible. According to this, the will is a dimension of consciousness. It is the latter insofar as it addresses the world intentionally. And here I agree with Sartre, with the addition that the will as an awareness of wanting to be in a particular way is an affirmation of one's own being in every action performed.

But I only partially agree with Fichte, because if morality, at least in the Fichte of the Jena lectures, consists in adapting the empirical will to the natural drive or pure will, then the latter must have content, and if it has content, not to realise it is to go against one's own nature. This cannot be admitted from the ontology of the forms of life, where every individual submits to a way of being by an act of self-imposition, and where being is understood here as the antithesis of any natural content identified with pure will. On the other hand, the acceptance of pure will implies accepting that there is a will prior to being, and we have said that being and will coincide. Pure will can only be will in another sense, in the sense of willing to will —in which the will coincides with itself and not with being. And as such, it can only be distinct from the willingness to be. So, the pure will as will-to-will has no content of its own, and although from the transcendental level it is configured as the possibility inherent in the will-to-be, phenomenologically it can be held as its condition of possibility only in retrospect, as that which is the negation of being, bearing in mind that one can only deny what is affirmed, and only with respect to what is affirmed, so that pure will as will-to-will can be held only through the constitutive opposite of being and precisely by means of the affirmation of being. That is to say, the self-affirmation of being, posits that which negates it, namely, its opposite, which, in turn, is its constant possibility. In short, if transcendentally, the possibility of being is found in the will-to-will inherent in the will-to-be, from the phenomenological perspective, our being is made possible by our opposite, that which cancels us out, from which we flee in order to be what we are. I expound on the will-to-will in Chapter Four.

On the other hand, Sartre thought that God was the *in-itself-for-itself,* the being that in itself has the reason for its being, which is taken as the ultimate goal of the human being (or human reality). From his perspective, of course, the human being could not be an in-*itself-for-itself.* 'The fundamental value which presides over this project is exactly the in-itself-for-itself; that is, the ideal of a consciousness which would be the foundation of its own being-in-itself by the pure consciousness which it would have of itself. It is this ideal which can be called God'.[29] However, there is no objection to considering the subject in this way if it is understood that he is the incarnation and progressive realisation of the form of life, which has in itself its *raison d'être* or foundation, as a non-natural entity, which is further defined as the totality of possible meaningful actions. So, as possibility, it is a totality; and as actuality, it is progressive totalisation. The unity is a totalising-totality. And it is the totality of possible actions with meaning; that is why it is an *in-itself-for-itself,* it is already what it is, a unity of principled actions —no meaningful action is outside of it. And only because of this, the subject can be its incarnation, i.e., what it is not —or is not yet— cannot be incarnated. So the subject is from the very moment of conversion already who he is as a possibility. This incarnation is that of a totality

---

[29] Sartre, *Being and Nothingness,* p. 566.

but in degrees of realisation by the subject. Nevertheless, he is already these possibilities, he is these possible actions with meaning, already a unit. He could not become who he is if this ontological unit, which is the form of life, was not posited as a possibility to be realised and if he did not want to realise it.

According to this, there are no instincts from which the form of life as will-to-be is derived. On the contrary, the will-to-be is always that of being a particular being with which one becomes a subject in a community. The child is born into a form of life. This implies actions that have a meaning of their own. The lack of instincts in human beings would mean precisely an expression of their unfinished character; this drives them relentlessly to endow their lives with a meaning of their own. Scheler wrote: 'The human being is the X that can behave "open to the world" to an unlimited degree. Becoming human is elevation to openness to the world by virtue of the spirit [self-consciousness].'[30] Instinct is pure, absurd, meaningless existence. Where instinct predominates, there is a lack of meaning, which only comes from the capacity for self-consciousness. The animal, which has no self-consciousness, cannot be aware of the meaning of its actions, as Scheler put it: 'The animal therefore has consciousness, unlike the plant; but it has no self-consciousness, as Leibniz has already seen. The animal does not possess itself, it is not master of itself; and therefore it has no self-consciousness either'.[31] Instinct leads us to isolated, disconnected behaviour, outside of a totalisation or project; it is the life of the chaotic multiplicity and the confusion of the senses –life without form-. The form of life in which the subject is born assimilates these instincts and transforms them into a meaningful totality, a being. Is it not what Heidegger points to when he wrote: 'Life, in its own right, is a kind of Being; but essentially it is accessible only in Dasein.'[32] Thus, the will is the consciousness of certain necessary behaviours. In the unity of the form of life, we must then complete Sartre's approach. We are not just consciousness, or preferably consciousness, but embodied consciousness, i.e., principled actions in the world.[33] The will-to-be is the consciousness of acts in accordance with the being that we are. That is the actions that we present to ourselves as necessary possibilities of our being. And as I develop below, our will is the affirmation of the being that we have given

---

[30] 'Der Mensch ist das X, das sich in unbegrenztem Maße "weltoffen" verhalten kann. Menschwerdung ist Erhebung zur Weltoffenheit kraft des Geistes'. In Scheler, *Die Stellung des Menschen in Kosmos* (Bonn: Bouvier Verlag, 1991), p. 40. Translation is mine.

[31] 'Das Tier hat Bewußtsein, im Unterschied von der Pflanze, aber es hat kein Selbstbewußtsein, wie schon Leibniz gesehen hat. Es besitzt sich nicht, ist seiner nicht mächtig -und deshalb auch seiner nicht bewußt'. In Scheler, *Die Stellung des Menschen in Kosmos* (Bonn: Bouvier Verlag, 1991), p. 41. Translation is mine.

[32] Martin Heidegger, *Being and Time* (Oxford: Blackwell Publishers, 2001), p. 75.

[33] Rebekka Hufendiek, *Embodied Emotions* (London and New York: Routledge, 2016).

ourselves and realise it through the consciousness of our actions. When the subject acts in the world according to his self-consciousness or anthropical image, he is exercising his will in the affirmation of his being. Thus, this conception shows that, contrary to Nietzsche and Schopenhauer, it is not instinct that moves us but a voluntarily self-imposed principle of being, which separates us from the instinctive life of animals. And on the other hand, contrary to Fichte, no pure will is required to explain the empirical will by which the individual bestows himself with being. This, however, does not deny the pure will in terms of will-to-will, but only shows the independence of the will-to-be from the instinctive force, which actually needs to be denied by the will in order to be, and that, in any case, the pure will is a will-to-will that does not determine behaviour at all, but makes the will-to-be possible and at the same time depends on it in order to persist as a will, because only by being a particular being can one continue to will. Thus, animals and plants, which exist but are not will-to-be, cannot change their life or perfect their existence. The absence of being limits them in their will. Finally, as mentioned above, it completes Sartre by overcoming his hierarchical dualism, whereby will is identified with consciousness; instead, will is to be thought of as the affirmation of a meaningful (principled) action. Will is the presentation of action as necessary, and ultimately the presentation of one's own being as necessary. It is the consciousness of one's own being as it carries out the actions demanded by its form of life. The will is thus the affirmation of the latter in each of his actions.

Why refer to the will as the beginning of the constitution of being as a form of life? We could be content to show empirical cases of various behaviours and then infer a kind of pattern and relate it to a group of subjects, perhaps statistically.... Or we could speak of a form of life without the need to descend to the will as the source and origin of its constitution... But the latter would mean seeing the trees but not the forest, not seeing the true transcendence of the will in the form of life. For the will is not only the origin, but what keeps us in our way of being and acting —as our subjective identity—, to the point that it could be said that we are what we want to be. However, we do not want all of what we are, because there is always a part that is in struggle and resistance with what we are made to be. We will have the opportunity to qualify this in the course of these pages, however, because it is true that it is not only our will that counts, but that it acts on a previous demand, the will of an other with whom we identify and whom we take as a subject to imitate —from the paternal-filial relationship to friendship and relationships of liking and admiration in general. The external will of the other exercised as a necessary imposition but without being understood as a possibility of one's own is never the origin of a form of life, it is only the origin of coercion, enforcement and a situation of resistance.

1.4. The Will is Political

The power of the form of life, or better, the form of life as power also informs us that all forms of life are political. But the 'political' must be defined and examined carefully. Let us deal with this aspect now in order to delimit and deepen below the onto-phenomenological sense in which the power of a form of life must be understood. We return then to the origins of political science. As has been discussed above, Aristotle defined man as *zoon politikon,*[34] that is, a political animal. And by *zoon politikon,* he meant that animal that is constituted within the polis as a community of rational discourse. In this sense, politics refers more to the postulated human essence of reasoning and the use of language in the agora than to relations of power in a general sense, for the Aristotelian idea of political community is that which 'aims at good in a greater degree than any other, and at the highest good',[35] and as later becomes clear the greatest good is a life according to the logos or rational speech, for this sets forth the values for the community. Thus he wrote: 'the power of speech is intended to set forth the expedient and inexpedient, and therefore likewise the just and the unjust'.[36] But to set forth the just and the unjust is political organization, for 'for the administration of justice, which is the determination of what is just, is the principle of order in political society'.[37] This political organization is essential in human beings, so through it, according to the Stagirite, the former realise their nature and perfect it. How are politics related to power, then? What links exist between both? This is the question that we are interested in dealing with here.

The first thing to bear in mind is that if the form of life is power, as I have assumed, politics must be in some way related to power, for the form of life is politics. That is to say, the way in which a subject or a community of subjects live can be understood as a political constitution and organization of life, for their behaviour emerges from their shared ontological principle, and fix what is to be human. Obviously, this goes beyond the Aristotelian postulate that states that 'man is by nature a political animal.'[38] So, we have to restate the Aristotelian definition. If indeed every subject is political, it is not because they have reason and language, nor because of their human essence. Every subject is political rather because every subject lives in a form of life; that is to say,

---

[34] Aristotle, *Politics,* in *Complete Works,* the Revised Oxford Translation, ed. by Jonathan Barnes, 2 vols (Princeton, New Jersey: Princeton University Press, 1995), II, 1253a pp. 4265-569.

[35] Aristotle, *Politics,* 1252a5, p. 4265.

[36] Aristotle, *Politics,* 1253a15, p. 4269.

[37] Aristotle, *Politics,* 1253a35, p. 4270.

[38] Aristotle, *Politics,* 1253a1, p. 4268.

against the Aristotelian accepted wisdom, the way in which the subject is political is due to his being a form of life more than to his being rational or animal possessing logos. Furthermore, he is political regardless of whether or not he contributes actively to the public life of his society as a sphere of dialogue and communication. And whether or not he is concerned with seeking the good of his collective life, as the only way to be regarded as good citizen and good man: 'it is not every citizen who is a good man, but only the statesman and those who have or may have, alone or in conjunction with others, the conduct of public affairs.'[39] For Aristotle, the human being is political because, by nature, he needs to live with others in order to realise his own nature, which leads to a circular argument: the being who is political by nature only by being political achieves his nature perfectly. But is this not a naturalistic fallacy? Since he is naturally political, he must remain so, for in the attainment of his telos or essence, there is a certain obligation or requirement expressed in the above quotation as the only state in which the human being can be good. But if by nature human beings necessarily tend to unite with others in a mutually beneficial community, why is this self-interested natural relationship (for no one is self-sufficient), which is portrayed as factual, then posited as the necessary prescription for the only way to be truly human? Or, in other words, if the good life, which is life subjected to the dictates of what is just and good in a community, is born of natural life, and this is a necessarily social life, for by nature, human beings tend to live in association, is not the good life —which is certainly political— presupposed and demanded in natural life? Must not human beings involve themselves in the public affairs of the community, for the common good, because that is what they necessarily do in the natural state when they associate with others in order to be self-sufficient together?

It seems that in Aristotle, nature is an explanatory resource at the beginning as well as at the end. And yet, according to him, one can live in society out of necessity without being good, that is, without fulfilling the human essence, but can one be good without living in society? It seems that his answer is negative, for 'who has no need because he is sufficient for himself, must be either a beast or a god'.[40] This implies a difference between the natural state and the political state, perhaps in that the former association is self-interested while the latter is moral, since it is a matter of seeking the good of the community and not just individual interest. But, if the life of natural association is necessary but not sufficient to be good, that is, to realise the human essence, would not the State which is removed from nature, either by defect (beast) or by excess (god), be in any case against nature. How is it then that human nature is fully attained by

---

[39] Aristotle, *Politics*, 1278b5, p. 4354.
[40] Aristotle, *Politics*, 1253a25, p. 4270.

the political state, which is taken for an unnatural state? Is it human nature that is fostered by political life or a particular type of human being according to the laws and principles imposed on his community? If what is being promoted is a particular way of being human, why insist that it be both genetically natural and unique in its essence? Is it not that insisting on continuity with the natural State is a way of legitimising what is in fact particular to each community and thus rather political or even cultural? But if it is the good man who is devoted to the common good and the realisation of human nature, why then assume a state of nature which, as argued, is in any case at best superfluous when not contradictory —seeking self-interested association— to the political state of seeking the common good, the good of the polis?

It seems that the Aristotelian explanation leads us to two inconsistent outcomes: either the end of the human being is already assumed in its natural origin, the prescription of political life being to elevate the description of the necessary and inevitable natural life to morality, so that it proceeds by means of a naturalistic fallacy, whereby it takes the ought for the being —or worse, it projects the ought into a supposedly factual state. Or else human beings surpass their strictly natural state by living under a community organisation that postulates what is good and just, so that by submitting to such a life, a certain perfection and goodness is achieved, which nevertheless cannot correspond to human nature, understood as the only way of being human, which has been overcome by ceasing to act in society out of individual self-interest, the motivation that had originally led them to associate in order to survive. Either naturalistic fallacy or *contradictio in terminis*. Therefore, it can be concluded that the subject is either political by living naturally in association or by living under laws and principles that constitute a community organisation beyond the said state of nature and make possible a particular way of being human. Furthermore, the first member of the disjunction is to be cancelled, for I claim that the subject is not political because he lives in society —that is, in association with others for a common goal—, considering that the hermit or anyone who lives in isolation continues to be political as long as he is the subject of a form of life, and even more intensely if he is in opposition and resistance regarding the hegemonic form of life of a given society as, for example, the thirteenth-century British hermit and mystic Richard Rolle, whose isolated life was taken as a dangerous counter-conduct by the Catholic Church to its own form of life imposed on society: 'The hermit, in his case, challenges the medieval Church's hierarchy in that hermits practice a form of living at a local level, placing them in dangerous, sometimes heretical, positions that force the Church to either absorb their practices or suppress them'.[41] In this sense, the form of life of a single subject is also possible and, even more so, taking into account that each subject aspires to its universal incarnation. The political then is strictly non-natural —not instinctive tendency— but rather has to do with the image of being human promoted by the community organisation imposed (and self-imposed by the subjects), bearing in mind that such organisation is the expression of the form of life, and this is as much the community's as the subject's, even if the subject is isolated or alienated from his community. For as I have argued elsewhere, a community does not necessarily have to be actual, although ideally should be, as this facilitates the co-imitation of its members and consequently their integration as subjects of their form of life.

Moreover, I conceive of a potential community as not only possible but necessary, for, in fact, there would be no actual community without a potential one, for it is not possible for one to be part of a community with which one shares nothing *a priori*, even if only *a posteriori* one becomes aware of this coincidence. In order for there to be coincidence in the way of doing, feeling and acting, this way must be prior to the encounter between the subjects. And this is contrary to Zahavi and Szanto's premises and well-reasoned, if not entirely convincing, arguments that only actual communities in which the members interact and get to know each other in a Me-Thou relationship are conceivable as such:

> It is a reciprocal exchange of address and response that affects and transforms the self-experience of the participating individuals (...) A we is constituted by me and at least one co-subject. But for me to relate to another co-subject is precisely for me to relate to somebody who not only has a perspective of his or her own on the world, but on me as well.[42]

I still think that, once the subject has been converted to a form of life —by the necessary conditioning or primordial external demand—, his community is all those subjects who share the anthropical image or principle of that form of life, and, for this very reason, these co-subjects need not necessarily know and interact with each other, just as in so far as they share a form of life, many of the citizens of a State or nation make up a community, and those who have been

---

[41] Christopher Roman, 'The Counter-Conduct of Medieval Hermits', *Foucault Studies*, 21 (2017), 80-97 (p. 81).

[42] Dan Zahavi, 'We in Me or Me in We? Collective Intentionality and Selfhood', *Journal of Social Ontology*, Published Online First (March 2021), 1-20 (pp. 16-17) https:// doi.org/ 10.1515/jso-2020-0076. See also Thomas Szanto, 'The Phenomenology of Shared Emotions. Reassessing Gerda Walther', in *Women Phenomenologists on Social Ontology*, ed. by S. Luft and R. Hagengruber (Switzerland: Springer Nature, 2018).

isolated in prison, as was the case with St. Paul, were still subjects of the incipient Christian religious community, even if he could not interact with them or know them all. Paul wrote in a letter from prison:

> Only let your manner of life be worthy of the gospel of Christ, so that whether I come and see you or am absent, I may hear of you that you are standing firm in one spirit, with one mind striving side by side for the faith of the gospel, and not frightened in anything by your opponents.[43]

Nevertheless, they all lived the same self-imposed form of life, some with more and some with less external conditioning and resistance. The latter would give rise to a discussion in parallel to that of Wittgenstein questioning the possibility of a private language, or better, the assertion of its impossibility;[44] but the comparison with the form of life would not be entirely appropriate, for in language one has an instrument of communication, and to communicate by definition requires another subject. And even if it is agreed that the way in which one understands oneself is intersubjective,[45] as it is in the ontological notion of form of life I am defending, still the others are in principle only posited, for my way of acting need not be shared by those who actually live in my environment. However, it is necessary to posit them as sharing the same way of being and acting, for my understanding of myself according to that way of being human depends on there being other human beings like me. That is, my understanding of myself is mediated by an intersubjective, and not merely individual, image, and to this, Wittgenstein's argument against the possibility of private language can be extended since, for him, all access to one's own consciousness would be intersubjective, although he would base such intersubjectivity on language and not on shared attitude and habits. Furthermore, the form of life as principled actions in the world is restricted if,

---

[43] *The Bible,* The English Standard Version (ESV), Philippians 1: 27-28. In New King James Version, (NKJV), it reads: 'Only let *your conduct* be worthy of the gospel of Christ, so that whether I come and see you or am absent, I may hear of your affairs, that you stand fast in one spirit, with one mind striving together for the faith of the gospel, and not in any way terrified by your adversaries'. In this version, the equivalent of a manner of life is conduct, which also presupposes a being led and being led (as Foucault points out).

[44] Wittgenstein, *Philosophical Investigations* (Oxford: Basil Blackwell, 1958), 1, §§ 138-242, also §§ 243-363.

[45] Karl-Otto Apel, *From a Transcendental-Semiotic Point of View* (Manchester and New York: Manchester University Press, 1998): 'In this linguistically founded assumption of the intersubjectively valid understanding of something lies the new paradigm for philosophy. For it follows therefrom that the never certain but still publicly intelligible (and with regard to criteria controllable and correctable) experience of the external world must assume a primacy over the subjectively private certainty of inner experience' (p. 125).

for example, one finds oneself in prison or in the midst of a society whose life principle and thus structural habits or —with Charles Taylor— 'social imaginary' is other than ours. But the image one has of oneself as the incarnation of a universal human being or anthropical image, it remains, and there is no reason why it cannot be shared with those who also incarnate it —maybe distant in time and space—,[46] even if it is, granted, in a deficient way as the one who is denied at his deepest core; which is precisely the guarantee that this behaviour proceeds from our very being.

Therefore, returning to our topic, the subject is simply political because he is the subject of a form of life. Let us say that here, the political indicates a relationship to the form in which that life is constituted. But at the same time, that form of life has its constituents, which are also structurally political, namely, the driving principle and the actions. But how exactly are these constituents political? In the first place, they are political because the principle demands a certain *way of being and acting.* What is more, it demands that being excludes anything other than itself. That's why the form of life is all that it is. But to be all that possesses being is tantamount to being a living political ideology. The principle of the form of life, moreover, as the law of the anthropical image that gives identity to the subject, is the affirmation of an exclusive way of being human. And that, too, is political in the sense here elaborated, that of organizing life. As Sartre put it: 'everyone is a non-human man for all Others, and considers all Others as non-human men, and actually treats the Other without humanity (...). These remarks, of course, must be understood in a proper sense, that is to say, in the light of there being no such thing as human nature'.[47] This judgement has to be understood as extended to the community through the notions I have been advocating of anthropical image and form of life, namely, *every community is a non-human community for all others.*

On the other hand, affirming oneself —through the principled actions— is political because it entails establishing limits. Limits, which mean determinations that the form of life imposes on itself in order to be a particular being. But they are also limits that exclude what cannot be included. It also designates a

---

[46] And as I said above, sharing here is possible if one thinks about the kind of principles and preferences that guide the actions of subjects, something like the social imaginary of possible behaviours guided by the same driving principle, such as the expectations and tendencies one has to seek silence and solitude to create art or to think philosophically, or the expectations and tendencies one has to act to maximise individual gain or community gain or the glory of God, or to maximise pleasure and well-being, or the greatest possible alienation and self-concealing, and so on. All these shared principles give rise to more homogeneous behaviour the more compact and actual the community is.

[47] Jean-Paul Sartre, *Critique of Dialectical Reason*, 2 vols (London and New York: Verso, 2004), I, p. 130.

rejection. Taking Ricoeur's analysis of the notions of 'recognition' and 'identification', to be could be said to self-identify with a way of being and to be recognised as such: 'what posits itself opposes itself insofar as it distinguishes itself, and nothing is itself without being other than everything else'.[48] This suggests that to be is to oppose that which is not like us. If what we are is defined by a particular anthropical image, all those who do not incarnate it to some degree will be opposed to us, they will be outside our community; they will be outsiders, that is, non-subjects. Those limits imply the power by which the form of life constitutes and finds itself. And that power is manifested through the acting, that is, through the subject's actions.

Therefore, contrary to how power has been usually defined in political theory, it is not primarily an imposition on others —in terms of 'a relation among people'—[49] but fundamentally on oneself. The form of life imposes itself, and the subject who incarnates it does too. The imposition on others is a consequence of the imposition on oneself. The political aspect of the form of life is a consequence of one's will-to-power. The form of life wants to be that particular being. That particular being that is the form of life affirms and universalizes itself by reinforcing its power of being. Thus, its power is an affirmation of its being. Being and power are one and the same thing. In the same way, affirmation and universalisation are ontologically linked. Power in relation to the political is, then, nothing more than the self-affirmation of the form of life as the organization and determination of life —a life which is simultaneous to its determination—. As I elaborate below, such self-affirmation includes the dimensions of identification, integration and foundation. But in what sense exactly can this affirmation of the form of life be taken as being political? We dedicate the following chapter to that question.

---

[48] Ricoeur, *The Course of Recognition* (Cambridge, Massachusetts: Harvard University Press, 2005), p. 27.
[49] That is exactly the definition of power according to Robert A. Dahl, 'The Concept of Power', *Behavioural Science*, 2 (1957), 201-15 (p. 203).

Chapter 2

Power and the Will-to-Be: Self-Affirmation

Our ontological investigation has already yielded some results concerning the characterization of power. The first thing we have identified has been the political organization and determination of life. And in that capacity, the political is identified with the form of life. And this is the affirmation of a particular being, not of Being in the abstract. Therefore, this affirmation is political, because it affirms a way of organizing and determining life. It is the will-to-be a particular being. And yet, the political is also defined with respect to power. But how should we understand power? *To be a form of life is to be political.* And to be political is the will-to-power. But the latter is equivalent to having power: The form of life has power. And when it affirms itself, it affirms its power with it. But power is not something material or a cause or an effect. Power IS, as the form of life IS. Now, to understand power from this ontology, we should reject all those groundless theories that assert a relationship between power and a material causality, be it the throne, lands, money, force, and so on. These are instruments that some subjects use to arrogate to themselves the power of the form of life, to be the perfect incarnation of the form of life as power.

Hence, some leaders have assumed the identification between the form of life and their person as a perfect incarnation. Thus, taking the State as the epitome of the form of life, a well-known French King, Louis XIV could say: 'I am the State and the State is me' (*l'etat, c'est moi*).[1] For he was the embodiment of the imposed form of life in his nation (see the chapter on Power, State and Ethics). Many political leaders promote a personal cult. And they do so precisely because they see in themselves the anthropical image with which all subjects must identify and realise through the self-imposed form of life. This cannot be understood as an abnormality. Quite the contrary. It is the ontological structure of the forms of life and of the subjects of it. The affirmation of the form of life is also done in each subject. Each subject, as a subject, tends to incarnate his form of life with perfection. Or, what is the same, tends to be integrated into the form of life through identification and imitation. Every subject, as a will-to-be and will-to-power, tends to want to say: 'I am my form of life' (i.e., I am a liberal

---

[1] Although reputedly he never said that, the sentence has been attributed to him since nineteenth century, and it fits well with his way of ruling as absolute monarch, see Joël Cornette, *La Mort de Louis XIV: Apogée et crépuscule de la royauté* (Paris: Gallimard, 2015).

democrat; I am a socialist; I am an artist; I am a philosopher; I am a scientist, etc.). And in this sense, he is prepared to defend it to the utmost, because his life is at stake. When the form of life is institutionalized through government's support as the legal and official life of the State, the leader, who incarnates that life more perfectly, wants to be able to say, 'I am the State'. Then, in the contemporary historical moment, we see that US President Biden, with his propagandistic slogan 'America is back', presents himself as the incarnation of America, which is held as the centre of the form of life of liberal capitalism and democracy, that is, the form of life of individual profit maximisation —which presupposes a moment of prior retreat hinted presumably at Trump—. And so it is with China, and the socialist or State capitalist form incarnated by Xi Jinping until recently: China is the Communist Party, and the Communist Party is Xi. The State concentrates the powers of a form of life when life is organized and determined by a government. The State and its leaders are the ultimate expression and incarnation of the form of life because they have competed with other subjects for it. We can call all these people the elites, and they are equal subjects of the form of life, although they are in a greater degree of integration and identification with it. These elites are also those who benefit most from such identification and integration. This is why they also have the greatest interest in its affirmation. Let us then deal with the relation between affirmation and interest, which is how the meaning of the form of life reflects on power.

2.1. Self-Affirmation and Interest

The will-to-be is driven by the ontological principle, which is not only motivation but also interest in its political dimension. This means that the affirmation of the self is also the affirmation of an interest. Interest is, therefore, how power is understood by the community and by the subject. It is how power appears before the consciousness of the subject. He experiences his power when he succeeds in realising his particular interests, and beyond them the fundamental one, that of being even more who he already is. The subject who has obtained, for example, the social status he was interested in through the work and remuneration he pursued, experiences in himself a certain power to achieve things, and thus experiences himself as that power, he feels powerful... This is the phenomenology of the fulfilled interest. And he has achieved not only something external, on the empirical level, through his actions, but on the transcendental level he has managed to bring himself closer to himself by affirming his anthropical image, and that is his major interest: to affirm himself, not necessarily in relation to another, which is rather an indirect consequence, but by affirming himself as more identical to himself, which implies a greater integration into his form of life, and thus into his community. The absolute-Other, the non-subject, is thus further away, while from the relative-Other, his co-subject, admiration is demanded. That is to say, the action that is driven by the principle, in its political dimension is an action driven by an interest, which, in relation to the organisation of life, we can properly call political action. For every organization pursue an interest. And to organize is in a sense 'to conduct', which can be as much to conduct others, let others conduct you or conduct yourself, as Foucault wrote: '"the way in which one conducts oneself [*se conduit*], lets oneself be conducted [*se laisse conduire*], is conducted [*est conduit*], and finally, in which one behaves [*se comporter*] as an effect of a form of conduct [*une conduite*] as the action of conducting or of conduction [*conduction*].'[2] Thus, to affirm the form of life is to affirm the subject in his political actions, which is, to conduct oneself as somebody else wants you to conduct yourself as well as to conduct yourself in the way you want others to conduct themselves. And thus the interest of every subject qua subject of a form of life is the same type of conduct. So, the interest in a particular way of being is also the interest in a particular way of acting.

The success of the subject in his particular interests must then be understood as political. Here, political action is not synonymous with participation in a government or its formation process. Political action must be understood as every action that the subject performs insofar as he affirms himself through his form of life. The political action of the subject always affirms an interest. And this interest is how power manifests itself. That is to say, power manifests itself in every action of the subject. Hence, there is no disinterested action from the point of view of the form of life. Not even that of a child, for as Heidegger already understood and rendered with his concept of 'thrown being-in-the-world' (*Entwurf*),[3] a child is born in a form of life as a totality of possibilities to be realised, that of his parents and probably of an actual community —which consists of co-subjects and not merely citizens of a society. His actions are mediated by it. The child identifies with the behaviour of his elders and this is undoubtedly taken as the behaviour that every human being must perform, i.e., he grasps a potential community where later the discourse of the actual community will make it equivalent to humanity and justify it as the only way of being human proper, and also as the good life.

Psychology tells us that 'in identification, the child is the primary active partner in taking-in and assimilating an adult's images and owning that

---

[2] Michel Foucault, *Security, Territory and Population. Lectures at the Collège de France 1977-78* (New York: Palgrave Macmillan, 2009), pp. 192-93.

[3] Martin Heidegger, *Being and Time* (Oxford: Blackwell Publishers, 2001), p.210: 'Is not Dasein, as thrown Being-in-the-world, thrown proximally right into the publicness of the "they"? And what does this publicness mean, other than the specific disclosedness of the "they"?'

person's ego and superego functions.'[4] And it distinguishes this from the complementary phenomenon, the depositing of the image parents have of what it is to be human in their children, which in turn begins to develop as his own image: 'In depositing, the adult is the primary active person who plants specific images into the developing self-representation of the child.'[5] A clear example of this identification of the child with the form of life into which he was born is the imitation it makes of adults, whom, in this precise onto-phenomenological sense, he admires, i.e., looks up to as role models. His imitation may seem unreal, as when the child imitates the father and puts an open book in front of him even though it is upside down and the child cannot yet read, or when he plays with others to buy and sell in an imaginary shop using stamps, pieces of wood or the parents' clothes —nowadays in this stage of digital capitalism it is certainly not wood or stamps or books that are used but mobiles—, nonetheless, this unreal is already the constitution of the child's consciousness and subjectivity, and I believe that in a sense it is the way in which the child tries to self-impose what in his or her form of life is a necessary possibility in order to realise the principle that drives him or her, be it economic maximisation or that of knowledge and intellectual life, etc. So, the power of the form of life is already perceived in such early behaviour or pre-habits of the child.

So, every action manifests the power that constitutes that form of life —as it perseveres in its being by affirming itself. The affirmation of power through action is governed by the will-to-be. Interest, in relation to the will-to-be, is, in any case, the interest to persist in being, to persevere and to perpetuate oneself. This perpetuation and persistence in being is political because it expresses the interest in continuing to be this form of life, of progressively integrating and necessarily founding oneself through it. This interest in continuing to be is, in turn, an expression of power or a dimension of the *conatus*, if you will. And this power is exercised over the form of life itself, by imposing itself to its subjects. It exercises a sort of demand of its own on its subjects, for they cannot fail to realise certain possibilities of action once they have self-imposed this form of life on themselves; these are the internal logical demands of its totalisation. But that imposition also affects what is outside of it. It affects it negatively. It limits it to a form of negativity.

The interest here is understood as the interest in remaining a form of life and remaining a subject of that form of life, which is also the interest in fleeing the denied realm that the forms of negativity consist of. Let us say that the subjects of a hegemonic form of life have an interest in persisting to be part of that form

---

[4] Vamik D. Volkan, *Immigrants and Refugees. Trauma, Perennial Mourning, Prejudice, and Border Psychology* (London: Karnac Books, 2017), p. 47.
[5] *Ibid.*

of life. And those who only imperfectly incarnate the form of life have an interest in becoming more integrated into it to the point of intensifying their identification through the interest in the form of life as such. By this I mean, on the one hand, those who, being within an actual community, have an interest in staying within it and prospering, and are thus actively involved and integrated, so that the owner of a small business is no less a capitalist than the entrepreneur of a large technology company, nor a layman any less religious than a member of the priesthood, and so on. What matters is the fundamental interest of the praxis of both, the interest in maximising, and thus making it all about business, or the interest in acting for the glory of a god. In any case, what moves them to identify with this image of human beings and their praxis is the correlative interest in the benefits of being so; being a capitalist or being religious is presented to the subject with benefits as well as with meaning, so that they wish to become more and more integrated. On the other hand, I refer to those who have had the experience of the migrant, understood as one who emigrates in search of a better life, and differentiating him from the refugee, who leaves his country forced by a situation that threatens his life and that of his family irreversibly in the short or medium term, or what David Miller distinguishes as an economic migrant (which I consider to be typical of the capitalist form of life) and a refugee:

> If we examine the profile of those who migrate into (and sometimes between) the liberal democracies, we quickly discover that by far the larger number count as economic migrants rather than as refugees (...) They are not driven out by a fear of persecution or some other immediate threat to their human rights, but drawn in by the advantages that their new society has to offer. Often the incentive to move is strictly economic.[6]

This economic migrant, even if they move from societies that are geographically distant from their destination, already share an image of human beings, some interests and, therefore, beyond administrative and security barriers, they belong to the same community, in this case mentioned by Miller, it should be attributed to the migration of the capitalist community; so that the Peruvian, Colombian or Mexican who arrives in the United States as an economic migrant, the same as the Moroccan, Algerian or Turk who arrives in the European Union, do so as capitalist subjects. That is to say, whether legally or illegally, they have the hope and the interest not to convert but to integrate and fully realise themselves as capitalist subjects, maximising their individual

---

[6] David Miller, *Strangers in our Midst. The political Philosophy of Immigration* (Cambridge, Massachusetts: Harvard University Press, 2016), p. 94.

earnings in a place where the conditions for such a form of life are better, and the resistance from other forms is lower. But this does not mean that these individuals were not already capitalist subjects; in fact, it is a presupposition that this is the case, since those who live frugally but without threat or danger do not emigrate; only those who have a capitalist interest translated as maximisation —of profits/human capital— emigrate, since, by various means, this form of life has become universalised to the point where it has become the hegemonic form of life worldwide. And this is shown by the fact that reverse migration, albeit minimal, also exists. I am referring to those who, living in the midst of a society whose majority community is capitalist, emigrate either to uninhabited places, as some Mennonites —hermits and tribes— have done, fleeing the consumerism and capitalist tourism of certain regions, or emigrate to societies whose hegemonic community is religious, such as Syria or Afghanistan. I leave aside as an extreme case those who have left Europe to join terrorist religious communities such as Isis or Al-Qaeda.

2.2. Interest and Disinterest

Another aspect to highlight with regard to the correlation between interest and affirmation is that of the dialectic between interest and disinterest. Interest in everything that integrates it and disinterest in everything that disintegrates it, paralyzes it and makes no sense for the subject. They are both correlates of affirmation and rejection. If by affirming its interest, the form of life affirms itself, in the same way, it does so by affirming its disinterest. All interest in persisting in its being carries with it a disinterest in that which is not its being. Disinterest in what it is not. Or in what is not yet. Here, the power of the form of life is also exercised as disinterest in the form of negativity. There is no interest in recognizing the being of something that denies one's being. In such a denial of the being, all the concealments of a form of life are founded. Its power is to assert itself as such a being. And for doing this, culture has been erroneously called soft power. Culture, as the institutionalization of a form of life, is the only and unique source of power. Any action, even warlike actions, come from its will-to-be and will-to-power. Everything that promotes its affirmation is driven by its interests. And by affirming its interest, it affirms its disinterest in that which constitutes its negation. The greater the threat, the deeper the disinterest. In every action, it affirms itself and denies the forms of life that threaten it.

If this is at the transcendental level, the experience of the subject is to be interested in that which affirms his subjectivity and identity (how his being appears to him) and to reject that which calls it into question or threatens it. But by the same token, he should also be interested in that which promotes his form of life and oppose or suppress that which endangers it. Byung-Chul Han has realised that in today's global capitalist society, the pursuit of sameness is reducing the encounter with the inherently different to the point of disabling genuine experience:

> The terror of the Same affects all areas of life today. One travels everywhere, yet does not experience anything. One catches sight of everything, yet reaches no insight. One accumulates information and data, yet does not attain knowledge. One lusts after adventures and stimulation, but always remains the same. One accumulates online 'friends' and 'followers', yet never encounters another person. Social media constitutes an absolute zero grade of the social.[7]

What seems necessary is an ontological foundation of this tendency to sameness beyond its description and the testimony of the aforementioned author. This dialectic I am referring to between the form of life and its negativity in the subjective experience of our daily lives explains why we reject behaviours and attitudes, as well as the agents who perform them, not necessarily because we find them negative in themselves, but because they do not align with our interest in life, the interest of the capitalist subject, in this case, since he does not need knowledge but data, he does not need friends but followers for his profit-maximising life project. For example, attitudes that express the driving principle of a greater harmony with nature, which implies a reduction in the use and abuse of its resources, cannot but be presented to the capitalist subject as something absurd from the outset, so that only if he receives pressure or resistance from other forms of life, he will adapt the ethical-propagandistic discourse to justify his actions and present them as convergent, but he will not change his pattern of action, because if he changes it, he will cease to be what he was, he will lose his meaning and that can only happen after a crisis and a profound conversion.

When I speak of the subject, I am referring to all the subjects of this capitalist community —all those who identify and affirm themselves with it— but fundamentally to the elites who are the ones who most intensely incarnate the interest of this way of being, acting and living. Is this not what we are experiencing in this second decade of the twenty-first century with the climate change summits, which are happening now more than ever, with the politically correct discourse of the shift towards green and non-fossil fuel energies? As can be seen, the question is in any case to find a substitute for energy resources while continuing to advance and integrate ourselves more and more into capitalist totalisation. Anything short of this is asking for a global conversion,

---

[7] Byung-Chul Han, *The Expulsion of the Other* (Cambridge: Polity Press, 2018), p. 12.

and the most active members of this resistance, with their slogan 'extinction rebellion'[8] demand it as a necessary shift -not always with a clear awareness of the magnitude of the change they are asking for- from all subjects of the capitalist community to the community that could be called harmony with nature, that which in its purest version can be attributed to the strict Buddhist life. This community has an interest that confronts that of the leaders of the capitalist world —the latter also presented in more positive tones, such as a global village. The subjects of this community also show the quasi-religious fervour of those proselytisers of Catholicism, Evangelism, and so on, who preached either conversion or doomsday and end of times. For in truth, every form of life exhibits the same onto-phenomenological structure.

The behaviour of the subject is the greatest expression of the power of the form of life. And if this is associated with a particular State because it is the State that has homogenised the behaviour of individuals around that form of life, institutionalised at the international level, then the affirmation that individuals make of their identity and subjectivity through their behaviour is the affirmation of both the form of life and that State. This means that in the subject is incarnated the power as an affirmation of what life has to be, supported by propaganda, but fundamentally, the power as a determination of what is worthy of interest. So, we can distinguish the interest in being, associated with the ontological principle, from the particular interests, associated with the actions and habits that constitute meaningful praxis. Again, it must be insisted that in a subject's behaviour, certain interests are expressed that only make sense within a form of life, and that defending that form of life and progressing in it is the fundamental interest that is at the core of a given action. In such an action, one would have to assume a power that is greater than that which the subject realises, a power that enables, motivates and directs all the subject's actions and interests. When the subject affirms himself, he affirms this higher power. This happens when in reflectively pursuing our own interests — sometimes called dreams— the interest of another is also realised. And the more I am myself, the more that Other is himself. But the subject does not usually become reflectively aware of that Other, which Lacan's psychoanalysis and later authors such as Žižek have called the big Other or 'the symbolic order as a consistent, closed totality".[9] That Other is the form of life in its totalising

---

[8] On its website, one can read: 'Traditional strategies like petitioning, lobbying, voting and protest have not worked due to the rooted interests of political and economic forces. Our approach is therefore one of non-violent, disruptive civil disobedience – a rebellion to bring about change, since all other means have failed.' In 'What is XR?' *Extinction Rebellion,* https://rebellion.global/ [accessed 28 October 2023]
[9] Slavoj Žižek, *The Sublime Object of Ideology* (London and New York: Verso, 1989), p. 77. Also, defined by Žižek as 'the alienating symbolic network' (p. 46).

principle or anthropical image.[10] When the subject triumphs with respect to its most intimate interests, this image of the human being also triumphs.

2.3. Interest and Self-Identity

According to the above, the subject, who seeks only to advance what he feels to be his innermost being, when he acts in a way that he can even call 'authentic' — without it being necessary at this phenomenological level to explore its authenticity— affirms himself as Other, that universal Other, which at the same time constitutes him and which he aspires to realise completely. The subject does not become reflectively conscious of this universal Other that constitutes him as the totality of his possibilities, but in each of the actions arising from this constitutive Other —this centre (*zentrum*)—, he recognises himself as someone he already was in some way, that is to say, there is this recognition of self-identity as 'selfhood'. With this, we resolve to discard self-identity defined as 'sameness' in the sense in which Ricoeur also questions it in *Oneself as Another*, that is, as an unchangeable Aristotelian substratum in relation to accidents. The French philosopher writes: 'Does the selfhood of the self imply a form of permanence in time which is not reducible to the determination of a substratum, not even in the relational sense which Kant assigns to the category of substance; in short, is there a form of permanence in time which is not simply the schema of the category of substance?'.[11] Ultimately, what the definition of sameness as substratum precludes is an inherent constitutive relationship between the self and the Other, as he acknowledges in explaining the title of his book: '*Oneself as Another* suggests from the outset that the selfhood of oneself implies otherness to such an intimate degree that one cannot be thought of without the other, that instead, one passes into the other, as we might say in Hegelian terms.'[12] Thus, the self I grasp in the reflection mode through my activity is given continuity by that non-posited Other —universal human being shared by my community— that makes my own action possible. That universal Other and I are not the same (there is between both not sameness), for I am not reflectively conscious of it, and, as my possibility, it cannot be reduced to what I am in the reflective mode. However, in each of my meaningful actions, that universal Other, which is my possibility of being and that of my community, manifests

---

[10] I think it necessary here to explain at least briefly the concepts I am using: this universal Other to which I refer is the non-posited Other of the anthropical image, that which constitutes the We or community, which in turn includes me and my co-subjects. The latter, with respect to my posited self are relative others, while the subjects of a different form of life are absolute others with respect to the We or community.

[11] Paul Ricoeur, *Oneself as Another* (Chicago and London: Chicago University Press, 1992), p. 118.

[12] Ricoeur, *Oneself as Another*, p. 3.

itself in the principle and interest that give continuity to my actions across time,[13] and more specifically, continuity across my totalisation, as a movement towards the future of my self-realisation —and posited foundation—, which is at the same time a permanent past, that of the universality of my possibilities.

For this very reason, if actions are directed by a particular interest, by carrying them out in their possibility, the subject recognises in himself a power of which he was not aware until he carried out the action. And with this power, this form of being human is consolidated by realising itself once again in the midst of the world. This conception of self-identity as selfhood or permanence throughout the totalising process of the subjectivization —Ricoeur's 'permanence in time'— does not explain how it is that we identify in the community and in the actions of others the same ontological principle. For, after all, there is a recognition in Others of the same way of being and acting. Our co-subjects are so because they have similar habits to us; they express their feelings in the same way, we share a way of doing and saying what concerns us, and so on. Moreover, we recognise in our own way of acting a continuity that we also find in them. However, we do not find this identity in all the individuals who make up our social environment; we do not identify with these Others, we do not recognise them in the way we do with our community of co-subjects.

If this is so, according to the ontological structure we have been developing, it seems that to identity as 'permanence in time', whereby the meaningful actions I perform are driven by the same principle, another notion of identity must be added in order to account for how our relative-Others, the co-subjects, are understood as such. This latter notion cannot but be that of identity as 'sameness', so that by comparison, I recognise in others the same identification. But how is it that we make use of this notion if we have discarded it at the beginning of this argument? While it is true that the concept of sameness implies an entity that is only said to be like another by comparison and is, therefore, an absorption of the same and a separation of the different and even rejection of the Other, the notion that we have accepted of 'permanence in time' cannot be formed as such without that of sameness. For if what remains in the process is the driving principle that gives us a continuous identity (e.g., one subject identifies himself as the one who glorifies God in his actions; the other receives his identity from his survival motivation, etc.), and the same is true for all those who share this principle, we still cannot explain why between such co-subjects there is identification. It seems that the solution lies in the fact that the subject compares the principle of his actions in the reflective mode with the principle of the actions of individuals whom he considers as co-subjects if there is an identification of principles and thus recognition of the

---

[13] Ricoeur, *Oneself as Another*, p. 117.

one in the other. This also seems to be Ricoeur's solution. However, for him, the union of both notions is through his proposal of narrative identity, which identifies an 'I' or subject that performs the action and maintains its identity in the story as a character with its goals or ultimate purpose in interaction with other characters: 'In narrativizing the aim of the true life, narrative identity gives it the recognizable features of characters loved or respected. Narrative identity makes the two ends of the chain link up with one another: the permanence in time of character and that of self constancy'[14]. To accept Ricoeur's thesis, however, with its emphasis on narrative, would imply misrepresenting the being of the form of life and the subject's actions in the world. As I have just revealed, there is an ontological way of explaining identity both as 'selfhood' and as 'permanence in time' without recourse to the narrative strategy. For, in the latter, identity ceases to be ontological and becomes one of linguistic signs.

On the other hand, the consequence of my thesis is that if certainly, as I have been showing, subjects are attracted to each other and reject those individuals who do not share their ontological principle, nevertheless, they themselves in their subjectivity are constituted by the universal-Other which is this principle as an anthropical image. The latter also constitutes its relative-Others, who are the co-subjects. So the subject and his community are not only constituted by the universal-Other, which gives them continuity in the process of self-realisation, but because of the latter, each subject can identify himself with the Other, who is his relative-Other and co-subject —for there is 'sameness' between them. This explains the exclusion that the absolute-Other has in the configuration of the world of a community, for, in a certain way, this arises from the fear of the difference, of not-being-who-one-is. Thus, by the ontological principle that governs our way of being and acting, our identity is configured as 'continuity in time', and by the similarity with the actions, tastes, emotions and values of another —which are governed by our same principle—, our identity can be taken as 'sameness'.

Even so, the question remains: what about those subjects who act not by identification and incarnation of this anthropical image or universal Other, but by a certain constriction or indeterminacy? Without even recognising it, the subject who acts in this way consolidates a universal Other, which is also his negation, since it is not the image of the human being with which he identifies himself and which constitutes him as his most intimate being. When we act, constrained by environment or necessity, or out of indecision, against our own sense of being —or meaning of life—, by our action, we are universalising that other image of human being, with its innate interest contradictory to our own, and

---

[14] Ricoeur, *Oneself as Another* (Chicago and London: Chicago University Press, 1992), p. 166.

with its power to impose itself on other images and assimilate them. This is the topic to which I dedicate the following section.

Chapter 3

Being and the Will-to-Power: Universalization

What has been shown so far is that the affirmation of the form of life in each subject is political not only as an expression of the will-to-be but also as an expression of the will-to-power —interest to persist in its being and becoming a more perfect version of it. While the affirmation of being is political because it determines what it is and delimits it from what it is not, the affirmation of being is also political as a will-to-power, because what it is, that is, the form of life, by affirming itself, imposes itself on itself and its subjects. The power of the affirmation of its being is precisely the affirmation of its power to be what it is: 'Every willing is a willing to be more. Power itself only is inasmuch as, and so long as, it remains a willing to be more power.'[1] Political actions are ideological because they precisely affirm a particular way of being and impose the conduct deemed necessary.

3.1. The Will-To-Power as a Political Will

The will-to-power of the form of life is imposition —through identification and imitation. Every imposition is a manifestation of power. Or rather, it is an exercise of power. As this imposition of the form of life is the imposition of its own being —as it is the subject's self-affirmation—, this exercise is that of having the power to be who one already is. That of imposing one's being on oneself. I advance that self-imposition refers to the actual being that the form of life as a totality imposes itself through its subjects, and, in particular, its elite. But the fact that it is an imposition on itself does not mean that it is not an exercise of power. Power here is ontologically delimited as constitutive of the form of life. And as constitutive of this, power is what separates it from other forms of life. For, by imposing its being on itself, in its pretension of universality, it negatively imposes its being on other forms of life, or rather on their non-being, for they are taken as *forms of negativity*.

In this latter sense, it is also this affirmation of being and will-to-power that makes the form of life emerge from its own possibility. So that the affirmation

---

[1] Martin Heidegger, *Nietzsche: The Will to Power as Art*, 2 vols (San Francisco: Harper, 1991), I, p. 60.

and its being are simultaneous but arise as the determination of the possibilities of being. This can be understood in a double sense. As an original sacrifice of the self-taken phenomenologically as a totality of possible possibilities or life as indeterminacy, by which the subject is born as a member of a community with the limited freedoms and necessary possibilities corresponding to a particular form of life. But it can also be understood as the sacrifice made of the possible Other as one imposes one's own being on oneself. For the other possibilities are not only discarded as possibilities but also as de facto becoming actualised by other communities, i.e., in the original sacrifice, certain possibilities have already been sacrificed from the outset with which the subject cannot identify and through whose suppression the subject can become what he is. In psychoanalytic theory, a movement similar to the one I have just described can be perceived with respect to the sacrifice of the subject in order to gain access to the social community. This is expressed by Žižek in *Enjoy your Symptom!*

> What is the entire psychoanalytic theory of 'socialization,' of the emergence of the subject from the encounter of a presymbolic life substance of 'enjoyment' and the symbolic order, if not the description of a sacrificial situation which, far from being exceptional, is the story of everyone and as such constitutive! This constitutive character means that the 'social contract,' the inclusion of the subject in the symbolic community, has the structure of a forced choice: the subject supposed to choose freely his community (since only a free choice is morally binding) does not exist prior to this choice, he is constituted by means of it.[2]

What the Ljubljana philosopher brilliantly points to in this paragraph is, precisely, that in this original sacrifice, the choice of the community in which one wants to be a member is a forced choice since the subject only emerges from this choice as a subject of a particular form of life. That is, the choice of community is something that occurs only once the individual has been constituted as a subject of that community; there is no subject prior to it, but both are simultaneous. This reminds us that the will is never alien to the involuntary, in Ricoeur's sense —commented on above— but neither is it suppressed by it. Rather, the original sacrifice is born of a free and spontaneous identification with respect to the possibilities offered by a primordial conditioning of the environment (empirical level of the form of life), which in turn is posited through the original image of being human. The affirmation is, therefore, subsequent to this identification with a way of being and acting to

---

[2] Slavoj Žižek, *Enjoy Your Symptom!* (London and New York: Routledge, 1992), pp. 74-75.

which we are exposed. The self-imposition of that being puts the subject on the path of integration and self-foundation. The political, in the will-to-power of the form of life, therefore, is the will to impose being on itself and its subjects: a political will, for the political has been defined as that which organises and determines the being of the form of life or the latter as being. This is why the affirmation in relation to the will-to-power cannot stop being political. It is precisely this political will to affirm oneself in a particular sense through certain ways of acting, feeling and valuing that would underpin the more sociological notion of 'governmentality' that Foucault uses to account for the normalisation operated by institutions and governments as galvanising the integration of subjects into the community.

> First, by 'governmentality' I understand the ensemble formed by institutions, procedures, analyses and reflections, calculations, and tactics that allow the exercise of this very specific, albeit very complex, power that has the population as its target, political economy as its major form of knowledge, and apparatuses of security as its essential technical instrument. Second, by 'governmentality' I understand the tendency, the line of force, that for a long time, and throughout the West, has constantly led towards the pre-eminence over all other types of power – sovereignty, discipline, and so on– of the type of power that we can call 'government' and which has led to the development of a series of specific governmental apparatuses (appareils) on the one hand, [and, on the other] to the development of a series of knowledges (savoirs). [3]

The difference is that the political will to which I refer, far from being pragmatic strategies implemented by the State and institutions with a view to the control and subjugation of the community, I hope to have shown by now that the coincidence of wills of the subjects within a community means the universal imposition of a being which is grasped as the only possible way of being, thus a necessary 'choice'. Because to impose one's being is to impose it universally, that is to say, it is to impose it as a universal with which one progresses in identification, which, in turn, constitutes the subject's identity and subjectivity. And this is not necessarily achieved under the auspices of the State and its

---

[3] Michel Foucault, *Security, Territory and Population. Lectures at the Collège de France 1977-78* (New York: Palgrave Macmillan, 2009), p. 144. Foucault also referred to a third element in his characterisation of governmentality, an element that I have left aside because it is too restrictive of a particular epoch. I reproduce it here: 'Finally, by "governmentality" I think we should understand the process, or rather, the result of the process by which the State of justice of the Middle Ages became the administrative State in the fifteenth and sixteenth centuries and was gradually "governmentalized." (p. 144).

institutions. In fact, originally, the subject and the community are prior to the State and the institutions of governance in a given society, since the imposition of particular practices does not in itself create a subject without the identification of the individual with the totality from which those practices emerge.

This ontological structure of universalisation gives rise to the inexorable tendency of subjects to proselytise —once divested this notion of its exclusively religious background—. This can be seen in every member of a group identified with a form of life, for all of us tend to posit pre-reflectively our way of being and acting —the only one we believe to be normal and good— on other groups, if anything, pretending to convert those who offer resistance, that is, trying to make others do, say and think like us. This is what is at the root of the dualistic distinction between barbarism and civilization. The following is Collingwood's definition of barbarism: 'By barbarism I mean hostility towards civilization; the efforts, conscious or unconscious, to become less civilized than you are, either in general or in some special way, and, so far as in you lies, *to promote a similar change in others'.*[4] I draw attention here in italics to the insistence on proselytising as a certain inherent aspect of the author's definition of barbarism —what one is, one propagates— which could equally be said of civilisation or of the subject supposedly considered to be 'civilising'. Thus, modern philosophy found a particularly early justification in Fichte, among others, when he wrote: 'the civilized must rule and the uncivilized must obey, if Right is to be the Law of the world'.[5] The civilized is always the one that follows an idea and it is the incarnation of Reason, for their form of life is the only one that has meaning for themselves. The Other, the uncivilized, must be shown the right road, that is, made to follow the civilized to become one. If this is not proselytism, what is? And this is a necessary dimension of the integrating process of a form of life. Because, as has already been argued, to affirm one's own way of being is to affirm that there is no other possible way, condemning the Other to barbarism, wrongness or inhumanity.

3.2. Universalization of the Form of Life as Universal-Particular

The universalisation of the form of life is a progress that responds to its internal need to be self-grounded. That is, to make its possibility fully necessary. And because it is necessary, unique and exclusive, universalisation is the imposition of its being on all its constituents and subjects. And ultimately to everything that is, since only within the form of life can one be. That is why, in order to be

---

[4] Robin George Collingwood, *The New Leviathan. Or Man, Society, Civilization and Barbarism* (Oxford: Clarendon Press, 1942), p. 342.
[5] Johann Gottlieb Fichte, 'The Characteristics of the Present Age', in *Popular Works*, 2 vols (London: Trübner & Co, Ludgate Hill, 1889), II, p. 49.

progressively more universal, the form of life has to gain in expansion. Universality, in this way, is also understood as incorporating into itself all that which previously was not by means of assimilation; to universalize means to impose itself, and to impose itself on other forms is to become universal through the affirmation of the other's negation. The latter signifies an essential change in the sense in which a subject understands himself, for by being assimilated, the subject is not only denied in his subjectivity but is given an alternative subjectivity, which is then sustained and affirmed in the negation of the previous one. For example, when capitalism assimilates the intellectual, it affirms him in its negative sign, as the opposite of intellectual life, i.e., ignorance, so that the more he maximises economically, the more he forgets himself and what he knows, and in his writings and works he propagates this ignorance, based on forgetting his own being, that which is driven by knowing himself as principle. The same with the subject whose purpose is to survive. When he is assimilated by the religious form of life, he becomes someone who affirms his being by maximising the glory of his god but through the negation of his previous form of life, the negation of the will-to-live as a principle, that is, through what Nietzsche calls decadence.[6] And so it is with other forms of life. In the process of universalisation, every form of life tends to absorb the Other, the forms of negativity, and thus to assimilate them into its negation. This means that the subject assimilated in the process of universalisation is integrated as a negated subject from the outset. Not only is the fundamental project of his life changed, but he is made to pursue it from assumptions contrary to those that constituted his previous subjectivity: the intellectual becomes ignorant, the religious becomes secular, the survivor becomes decadent, the artist becomes a copyist, the frugal and austere becomes a profit-maximiser or capitalist, and so on.

The result of the universalization process within a given and delimited society is what can be called hegemony proper. The latter has been widely discussed in social theory and political philosophy since at least Gramsci and later with Raymond Williams. Both refer to the superstructure of society, and in particular to culture and ideology over and above economics and politics. Hegemony refers to the culture or ideology of the dominant class that imposes itself on the others; in Raymond, it refers to the plurality of cultures and the relations between them, which refer to diverse social groups according to profession, origin, race, etc., rather than to classes, which would be Gramsci's original analysis, as dominant and dominated class. What is important to analyse now is how a form

---

[6] Friedrich Nietzsche, *The Will To Power*, ed. by Walter Kaufmann (New York: Vintage Books, 1968): 'A kind of self-destruction; the instinct of preservation is compromised. — The weak harm themselves. —That is the type of decadence.' (p. 28).

of life is at the same time universal and particular, and how, by imposing itself on those other forms of life with which it comes into contact, it becomes hegemonic in a given space. Contact can be between individuals incarnating different forms of life, between small communities within a society, or between States and even between alliances of States.

Universality in relation to hegemony was understood in the early twenty-first century by Ernesto Laclau in his dialogues with Slavoj Žižek and Judith Butler as embodied in the particularity of a group: 'there is hegemony only if the dichotomy universality/particularity is superseded; universality exists only incarnated in —and subverting— some particularity but, conversely, no particularity can become political without becoming the locus of universalizing effects'.[7] This can be equated with what I have been considering as the universality posited by a community incarnating a particular anthropical image. The reason why universality needs particularity is, according to Laclau, 'because universality cannot be represented in a direct way —there is no concept corresponding to the object'.[8] And yet, he infers, if it is necessary for the universal to be represented by a particular in order to establish itself as hegemony, because the universal cannot be grasped by itself, it is only the representation of an impossibility, which inevitably gives rise to a 'distorted representation'. And he concludes that, by the same token, the representation of the universal cannot but be 'constitutively inadequate', since it is realised by 'particularities which, without ceasing to be particularities, assume a function of universal representation'.[9] The universal, therefore, manifests itself, albeit to a limited extent, in the particular.

The analysis, in general, seems adequate, and yet it is easy to question it from the perspective of the forms of life. In order to do so, a distinction must be made between the universal and the 'universalisation' of the universal. This is something that, although it naturally follows from my analysis, has also been defended by Judith Butler in the following terms: 'By reserving the term "universalization" for the active process by which this contest proceeds, and "universality" for specific contenders for the hegemonic claim, this first term exempts itself from being one of the contenders, and seems to supply a

---

[7] Ernesto Laclau, 'Identity and Hegemony: The Role of Universality in the Constitution of Political Logics', in Judith Butler, Ernesto Laclau y Slavoj Žižek, *Contingency, Hegemony, and Universality* (London and New York: Verso, 2000), pp. 44-89 (p. 56).
[8] *Ibid.*
[9] *Ibid.*

framework within which all contention takes place'.[10] For my analysis, the former refers to the particular way of being of a community as it aspires to merit the universality that constitutes it; the latter has to do with the expansion of that universality by which it tends to embrace other particularities, which are now assimilated. Hegemony is not, therefore, the universal per se, as Laclau seems to identify, but rather the universalisation of a universal within the margins of a society. The hegemonic responds to a social group, while the universal responds to a form of life. The particular requires the universal as much as, conversely, the universal requires the particular; but the universal is not unique, which is again what emerges from Laclau's argument, and perhaps even from Žižek with his Lacanian notion of the 'primordial lack' or 'barred subject'.[11] The universal is the condition of possibility of the particular, so that the latter presents itself as universal by ontological necessity, just as another particular, another community, represents its own universal. To impose oneself as the only universal within a given social framework is what I believe to be hegemony.

So, as I said above, the universality that universalises itself into hegemony has had to sacrifice all other universals in what Butler has called 'competing universalities' in the text with the same title. To this end, she takes social movements as universals, although she identifies them with their propagandistic slogans, in a concession to the discursive that I believe leads to misunderstandings, and not with the ontological constitution of these movements as members of a community and an alternative form of life, such as the climate change or social equality movements: 'social movements may well constitute communities that operate with notions of universality which bear only a family resemblance to other discursive articulations of universality. In these cases, the problem is not to render the particular as representative of the universal, but to adjudicate among competing notions of universality'.[12] And, as a corollary of this, if the particular is the impossible representation of the universal, it is precisely because of the concept of representation used by Laclau, which is fundamentally epistemological, in the manner of *the regulative*

---

[10] Judith Butler, 'Competing Universalities', in Judith Butler, Ernesto Laclau y Slavoj Žižek, *Contingency, Hegemony, and Universality* (London and New York: Verso, 2000), pp. 136-81 (p. 164).

[11] Slavoj Žižek, 'Class Struggle or Postmodernism? Yes, please!', in Judith Butler, Ernesto Laclau and Slavoj Žižek, *Contingency, Hegemony, and Universality* (London and New York: Verso, 2000), pp. 90-135 (p. 9).

[12] Butler, 'Competing Universalities', p. 163.

ideas of reason (Kantian ideas of God, World, Man);[13] this universal cannot be the object of thought, but it is necessary in order to be able to think.

However, if the universal were thought of as the principle which is the condition of possibility of the particular, there is no need for representation, because every particular is itself such a universal, just as its constitution is eminently universal, that of pre-reflective consciousness or original self-consciousness. And if instead of epistemologically or what Butler calls 'universality as a purely logical category', it is understood from the standpoint of praxis, the universal is the way of being and acting —inevitable, as arising from the very constitution of its subjectivity— that a particular community exhibits in a manner limited to concrete situations and cases. The universal is not represented as if it were a scale drawing of a landscape; the universal is incarnated in activity; it is action itself. By this, he means that it is not a question of displacement from something that is particular and determined to a universal mode of presentation. They are not two levels external to each other, but the universal is the framework or totality of the possibilities of the particular, or in other words, the particular is the universal realised and incarnated in the midst of the social world, thus redefining the two levels advocated by Žižek: 'a certain historical horizon and the more fundamental exclusion/foreclosure that grounds this very horizon.'[14] That is to say, the unity of the transcendent-immanent or historical, as Butler defines it:

> In the Kantian vein, 'transcendental' can mean: the condition without which nothing can appear. But it can also mean: the regulatory and constitutive conditions of the appearance of any given object. The latter sense is the one in which the condition is not external to the object it occasions, but is its constitutive condition and the principle of its development and appearance. *The transcendental thus offers the criterial conditions that constrain the emergence of the thematizable.*[15]

According to this, then, the social group that presents itself as the universal and measure of society is the particular group or community whose universal has imposed itself as the universal way of being and acting on the rest of the communities in society —an imposition which it will justify with discourses

---

[13] Immanuel Kant, *Critique of Pure Reason,* translated and edited by Paul Guyer and Allen Wood (New York: Cambridge University Press, 2000), A643-A668, pp. 590-604.
[14] Slavoj Žižek, 'Class Struggle or Postmodernism? Yes, please!', in Judith Butler, Ernesto Laclau and Slavoj Žižek, *Contingency, Hegemony, and Universality* (London and New York: Verso, 2000), pp. 90-135 (p. 108).
[15] Butler, 'Competing Universalities', p. 147.

that are otherwise empty—. The latter —other communities— can only remain as resistance, but it can do so precisely on the basis of its status as universal. For while the particular historical realisation may be foreclosed occasionally, their possibility of persistence is due to the universal they incarnate. Thus, even if I am forbidden to act as I wish or prevented from acting in that way, I am still my own possibility of being and acting, and so I will realise myself according to it whenever I can. Hegemonic power, therefore, acts on this possibility. This is not the possibility of actions regulated by institutions and the State, as Foucault understands it, that is, 'a set of actions brought to bear upon possible actions'.[16] Rather, it is the possibility that constitutes the identity and being of subjects, and that ultimately springs from their will, as it has been shown in the introduction to this book.

3.3. Universalization, Hegemony and Politics: The Kynical Resistance

Thus, in the struggle for hegemony, at least two ways of being human confront each other. And here, we must bring back the notion of politics that we have discussed in previous sections. For that universal is always a political universal insofar as it organises and regulates the life —the habitual behaviour— of subjects and limits, marginalises, punishes or expels non-subjects who persist in their 'non-being'. But such attitudes are primarily those of the subjects themselves towards non-subjects; it is not governments or institutions that are the original causes but the form of life they have incorporated, and ultimately, the subjects that make up these institutions and States as members of communities that tend towards proselytisation and universalisation. There is no need for a State that inspires rejection of the other; every subject as the subject of a way of being and acting rejects those who resist that way, except on rare occasions of generosity, which I briefly mention further below.[17] Such a refusal is always political because it is about defending a way of living, which refers to those basic attitudes —feelings and discursive valuations— and habits constitutive of the community with which the subject identifies.

The latter can be seen clearly in the movement that is proliferating among young people in capitalist countries (originating in China), the so-called 'Lying flat' (*tǎng píng*) movement, according to which its subjects want to break with all the expected and necessary habits of those who identify with the capitalist community: members of this other, growing community do not work and are not willing to work in the proliferating precarious jobs —the 'bullshit Jobs'

---

[16] Michel Foucault, 'The Subject and Power', translated by Leslie Sawyer, *Critical Inquiry*, 8:4 (1982), p. 789.

[17] In the conclusion of this book I return to the notion of generosity.

described by anarchist anthropologist David Graeber—,[18] do not consume, do not socialise, do not expect high pay and do not expect to climb the social hierarchy of professions and trades, reject economic-based social status, and defy the pressure and stress of the capitalist community and its institutions. In short, as one of their champions, Luo Huazhong, writes in his blog, what they stand for is their 'right to choose a slow lifestyle'.[19] It is not by chance that they take Diogenes the Cynic, whose form of life could be understood as a search for contentment in frugality and precariousness, as a historical and philosophical reference for their movement.

This contemporary recovery of this form of life seems to signify the identification of some subjects with the antipodes of the capitalist form in which they are unwittingly immersed. They represent that form of negativity that can be formulated as the ghost of capitalism, its constitutive negativity. Thus, this dissident community is perhaps the real *bête noire* of any capitalist society and, perhaps, the only true revolution in it, even if it is now only in its infancy —though it is already beginning to spread to Western societies in the post-pandemic world— one can discern a future of either early absorption by the capitalist community which will eventually assimilate it to its 'need' to maximise, or the beginning of the end of this hegemony of the principle of economic maximisation. This resistance is, first and foremost, the feeling of subjects who cannot but actualise this way of being and acting —it is their *necessary possibility*— having constituted their world and their subjectivity with the form of negativity that they have swept up in the hegemonic form of life from which they spring.

Contrary to Hegel, who considered that Athenian cynical 'way of life was (…) not independent, but merely a consequence of these social conditions, and

---

[18] David Graeber, *Bullshit Jobs* (New York: Simon & Schuster, 2018).

[19] Cassady Rosenblum, 'Work is a False Idol', in *The New York Times*, 22 August 2021. This movement, like others born in the age of digital capitalism, has expanded through social forums —the most effective way of making proselytes in these decades. Those who resist like the 'Lying Flat' subjects, although their resistance is based on affirming the way of being and acting with which they identify (non-maximisation and instead contentment in precariousness), also tend to proselytise, and their integration and consolidation as a current form of life and community also depends on their -universalist- proselytising. As it is recent, there are no studies or reports yet on this movement, but one can read newspaper articles such as the one that appeared in *The Guardian* ('The low-desire life: why people in China are rejecting high-pressure jobs in favour of "lying flat"'. *The Guardian*, 5 July 2021, accessed 28 October 2023) and the reaction of the Chinese communist party through its information agency *Xin Hua* ("'躺平'可耻，哪来的正义感?" ['Lying flat' shameful, where is sense of justice?] *Xinhua*, 20 May 2021).

itself an unprepossessing product of luxury',[20] in this case, the reaction seems to be not so much to the historical social conditions as to the principle that moves and produces those conditions: *the reaction is the affirmation of the constitutive negativity of the capitalist form of life*. This is, on the other hand, the path pointed out decades ago by another cynical follower of Diogenes, the German philosopher Peter Sloterdijk, with his *Critique of Cynical Reason*, who distinguished between 'kynicism' and 'cynicism', defining them in the following way: 'The first is the motif of self-preservation in crisis-ridden times, the second a kind of shameless, "dirty" realism that, without regard for conventional moral inhibitions, declares itself to be for how "things really are"'.[21] And it understands it as the life philosophy of a society in crisis, such as today's global capitalist society or 'World village'; its directives are surprisingly similar to those of the new 'Lying flat' movement:

> Periods of chronic crisis demand of the human will to live that it accept permanent uncertainty as the unchangeable background of its striving for happiness. Then the hour of kynicism arrives; it is the life philosophy of crisis. Only under its sign is happiness in uncertainty possible. It teaches moderation of expectations, adaptability, presence of mind, attention to what the moment offers. It knows that the expectation of long-term careers and the defense of social assets must entangle one in an existence 'as care' (*sorge*).[22]

In this quote appear the watchwords of the new community of subjects that are established in the negation of capitalism: moderation of expectations or what I have called frugality and contentment with the present, adaptability rather than dreaming of a stable job or career, presence of mind rather than the stress

---

[20] Georg Wilhelm Friedrich Hegel, *Elements of the Philosophy of Right* (Cambridge: Cambridge University Press, 2003), sec. 195, p. 231.

[21] Peter Sloterdijk, *Critique of Cynical Reason* (Minneapolis and London: University of Minnesota Press, 2001), p. 193. It must be stressed that the self-preservation of the *kynical* (with K) here is not exactly that of biological survival but rather as the subject of a community in a hostile or suppressive social context; on the other hand, the *cynic* (with C) is associated with those who impose and justify their form of life, with its inherent necessary behaviours, as the way things really are (*c'est la vie*), that is, what I have been formulating in terms of imposition as necessary and unique of a form of life that is merely one of the possible ones: one of the images of being human. Such cynicism, however, does not necessarily have a duplicity or a fallacious intention on the part of its subjects, the fallaciousness would be in the very self-imposition of such a way of being and acting as the only one, but once such an imposition has been made, the subject is perfectly authentic when he acts according to it and discursively justifies it as proper to human nature.

[22] Sloterdijk, *Critique of Cynical Reason*, p. 124.

and rapid concatenation of maximising desire under capitalism, attention to what the moment offers or fruition of the present, which boils down to the rejection of both long-term careers and social assets —and social status, I would add— because both integrate or assimilate the subject into a world that he does not feel is his and therefore for which he cannot care and for which he does not want to show care (*sorge*). Is not the subject of the 'lying flat' movement then, in the best of senses, a kynical rather than a cynic? For, like the kynical, the 'lying flat' subject has also decided not to live in a form with which he does not identify; his resistance is his way of being, and can be described as 'lying in the sun, observing the goings-on in the world, being glad, and having nothing to wait for'.[23]

Proselytism, in the ontological sense, is the universalisation of the being of the form of life. Every subject, insofar as he is, is also a proselytizer. He seeks the ultimate universalisation of his form of life. Because only with his ultimate universalisation can the subject be a subject. This means that for the subject to be that universal subject, the non-subjects with which he encounters must also become subjects. Sharing with all subjects his form of life is his way of continuing to be a subject, and, therefore, of continuing to be what he is, his identity. The intrusion of a non-subject clouds universality, because, as a non-subject, he is a possible subject —by his very condition of not being one. But, if possible, it is also necessary in his always possibility of being a subject, according to the integrating and universalizing process of the form of life. This is the basis of proselytism. Every such subject is necessarily a proselytizer. A subject that seeks to universalize his being, because if it were not universalized, it would be in potentiality denied as such. Heidegger wrote about the will to power of being ever more: 'Only by means of perpetual heightening can what is elevated be held aloft. Only a more powerful heightening can counter the tendency to sink back; simply holding onto the position already attained will not do, because the inevitable consequence is ultimate exhaustion'.[24] Universalisation is structural and necessary.

This can be better understood if one thinks again that universalisation lies in the necessary identification with an anthropical image as the only way of being human, or if you will, the only way of being. Proselytism is rendered then as cultural expansionism, colonialism and imperialism. This means that all forms of life tend structurally to a certain expansion of themselves into the other. Or rather, a certain capacity to incorporate what it is not into its own being. For in

---

[23] Sloterdijk, *Critique of Cynical Reason*, p. 159.
[24] Heidegger, *Nietzsche: The Will to Power as Art*, p. 60.

this way, the non-being becomes being in the sense given by Fichte to the ontology of human beings in the *Vocation of Man*:

> In every moment of his existence he tears something from the outward into his own circle; and he will continue thus to tear unto himself until he has devoured everything; until all matter shall bear the impress of his influence, and all spirits shall form one spirit with his [...] Such is man: such is everyone who can say to himself: I am man.[25]

Otherwise, the threat that non-being persists in its state, as has been mentioned with regard to the subject, consists in the form of life not reaching complete universalisation. For, although its universality applies to everything that is, insofar as it is principled by it, what it is not —that is, the form of negativity—, manifests itself negatively at the same time as a resistance regarding being and as its possibility. And, therefore, as a resistance to the being of the form of life and a possible assimilation. This last one is due to the fact that being in its structure tends to its universalisation. That is, the tendency of a concrete being towards the universalisation of its principle of being and its interest. Opposed to this tendency towards universalisation are the other forms of life, the other universals —incompatible with each other, if you like. The latter, which also tend towards such universalisation, resist. But such resistance is not as in Foucault, where it seems that their mode of being is simply to resist, that is to say, as if 'counter-conduct' or even the 'critical attitude' —by which the French author replaces the former notion from 1978 onwards—[26] only exists as a reaction to hegemonic behaviour that is imposed through normalisation devices. Lorenzini explains it as follows: 'Foucault's insistence on the otherness that characterizes these counter-conducts is not accidental: resistance, in fact, never arises in a vacuum but is always relative to something or someone — resistance always aims at changing, modifying, transforming a specific situation, in order for the individual to be conducted (or to conduct him/herself) autrement'.[27] From the exploration of the ontological structure of the forms of life, it must be understood that to resist is to exercise one's own power of being as will-to-be and will-to-power.

---

[25] Johann Gottlieb Fichte, *The Science of Knowledge* (London: Trübner & Co. Ludgate Hill, 1889), pp. 334–35.

[26] Daniele Lorenzini, 'From Counter-Conduct to Critical Attitude: Michel Foucault and the Art of Not Being Governed Quite So Much', in *Foucault Studies*, 21 (2016), 7-21 (p. 8): 'starting from *What is Critique?* [May 1978, at the Société Française de Philosophie], Foucault seems to replace the notion of counter-conduct with the notion of critical attitude'.

[27] Lorenzini, 'From Counter-Conduct to Critical Attitude', p. 11.

According to the latter, resistance is nothing more than the community's affirmation of its own being, even if it is an occasion for reflective self-consciousness. This affirmation, on the other hand, implies a subjectivity that is in action but also transcends it. This differs from Foucault in that the French author understands normalisation and resistance in fundamentally behaviourist terms, of institutions and States that impose or favour certain practices and obliterate others: 'so we have two series: the body-organism-discipline-institutions series, and the population-biological processes-regulatory mechanisms-State. An organic institutional set, or the organo-discipline of the institution, if you like, and, on the other hand, a biological and Statist set, or bioregulation by the State'.[28] Moreover, it should be added that counter-conduct, according to the Foucauldian concept, is only counter-conduct from the perspective of hegemonic power,[29] which then perceives it as an object and not as part of the process of subjectification of its universal community. This thing that manifests itself in resistance to the attempt to posit the hegemonic universal is a thing that in itself is neither understood nor can it be granted the status of being. For that it has to be assimilated.

The latter leads us to confront the question that, as a starting point, brings into dialogue the three philosophers I mentioned above, Butler, Laclau and Žižek, namely, how is political hegemony possible and what struggles are required to achieve it?[30] In the discussion above, I have already briefly analysed how hegemony is possible and even necessary and inevitable. On the other hand, we are witnessing how capitalist life has become hegemonic on a global level. Although Butler explicitly denies the appropriateness of Hegel's —and as

---

[28] Michel Foucault, *Society Must Be Defended. Lectures at the Collège de France 1975-1976* (New York: Picador, 2003), p. 250. And Butler reveals how these institutional actions, according to Foucault, express an almost mechanical or alchemical process by which they create a subject out of the destruction of his body: 'The body is not a site on which a construction takes place; it is a destruction on the occasion of which a subject is formed. The formation of this subject is at once the framing, subordination, and regulation of the body, and the mode in which that destruction is preserved (in the sense of sustained and embalmed) in normalization.' In Judith Butler, *The Psychic Life of Power* (California, Stanford: Stanford University Press, 1997), p. 92.

[29] From what has been said in these lines it follows logically that what for hegemonic power is counter-conduct, for the resisting community does so through their behaviour, theirs is not counter-conduct but the way in which these subjects conduct themselves. Moreover, from this we can also infer that any behaviour that is literally a counter-conduct, i.e., a reaction to the imposition of a normalised behaviour, becomes chained to and dependent on that behaviour, without which its counter-conduct could not be interpreted as such. In the end, this counter-conduct, which is a reaction, is in reality a reinforcer of the hegemonic behaviour, which is thus legitimised.

[30] Butler, 'Competing Universalities', p. 159.

shown above, first of all, Fichte's— notion of *Aufhebung*, that is, the 'monolithic and carnivorous Hegel whose "Spirit" incorporates every difference into identity',[31] not only seems to me to be the most adequate understanding of how hegemony is achieved, but otherwise there could be no question of hegemony or the struggle for hegemony. In fact, Butler's proposal to translate from one universal to another by making clear the advantages of one over the other seems to me, if important, also insufficient, because it moves only at the level of rational discourse, with which to convince of what there may be in common in the demands of opposing universals:

> It will be the labour of transaction and translation which belongs to no single site, but is the movement between languages, and has its final destination in this movement itself. Indeed, the task will be not to assimilate the unspeakable into the domain of speakability in order to house it there, within the existing norms of dominance, but to shatter the confidence of dominance, to show how equivocal its claims to universality are, and, from that equivocation, track the break-up of its regime, an opening towards alternative versions of universality that are wrought from the work of translation itself.[32]

If the objective here is to translate between the different demands of movements of the same political tendency, such as the Left, the question would be: how is it attributed to being left-wing from the outset? For in this attribution, a common principle must be identified, which is also the one that must give them universal unity and presumed hegemony. Those movements can, therefore, only be considered left-wing if one assumes what the fundamental, practical and ideological principle of the left-wing subject is, and more specifically, what its form of life is. Can one be a left-wing capitalist? Does being left-wing correspond to leading one's own form of life different from that of those who are not? Is being left-wing to be concerned about the social conditions of the community? And is that not deciding and acting to maximise the collective benefits of the community? Is the latter perhaps being left-wing? If so, is the community to be understood as all the subjects with whom one identifies or all the individuals of the social group, of the country, of humanity? After all, to pursue hegemony is to pursue the change of the form of life of other communities. Would the left seek to convert all those who do not live as they do in order to be able to maximise the benefits of these, too, bearing in mind

---

[31] Butler, 'Competing Universalities', p. 174.
[32] Butler, 'Competing Universalities', p. 179.

that every universal cannot but be particular at the same time? Does the left seek to maximise the benefits of those who live as capitalist subjects?

In any case, if we refer to a hegemony that is not only left-wing but made up of many other communities, it is not enlightened reasoning that would convince these communities to change their form of life and their being —for example, the tribes of the Amazon and the aborigines of Australia, or the thousands of monks and peasants who live in seclusion and isolation in their rural and religious communities respectively— to become full capitalists. To translate from one to the other universals —in the sense of lived universals— is, in any case, to misrepresent both, for their respective demands are not isolated but internally cohesive by irreconcilable principles and mutually exclusive wills to be. One and the same demand such as *equality* can mean 'distributive or outcome equality' for a community of 'collective maximisation' such as some tribal societies, communes and phalansteries, while it can mean 'equality of opportunity' for a community of 'individual maximisation' such as the capitalist one. The constitutive ontological principle, like Lacan's *point de capiton*, [33] necessarily reorganises its demands and actions. Demands are certainly not mere language but lived experience and attitude in the world. Both equal, but also both at odds with each other. Hegemony —global as well as regional or local— is achieved by taking into account the two essential pillars of the form of life that is the object of change: the constitutive principle of consciousness and habitual actions.

I agree with Butler here, but adding something important, it seems to me: they are not rational discourses where the advantages of one over the other or what they have in common is brought to the front, even in the supposedly universal demands of the left and its social movements, as these could even respond to contrary forms of life such as the 'Austerity Movement' (2005), a clear example of capitalist subjects aspiring to a maximisation of profits and economic status that, nevertheless, seems unattainable, hence their frustration. The discourses that promote hegemony are rather counter-discourses, or counter-propaganda, i.e., those discourses whose primary purpose is to create doubt in the subject with respect to his form of life, an agonising doubt that weakens his will to persist in his being and accede to conversion into the form of life that thus denies him. It is not a rational debate, but rather a persuasion aimed at the will of the subject.

---

[33] Slavoj Žižek, *The Sublime Object of Ideology* (London and New York: Verso, 1989). The latter wrote: 'the multitude of "floating signifiers", of proto-ideological elements, is structured into a unified field through the intervention of a certain "nodal point" (the Lacanian *point de capiton*) which 'quilts' them, stops their sliding and fixes their meaning.' (p. 95).

Propaganda is always political precisely because it affirms one form of life and rejects its opposites, those that resist it. The purpose is always to weaken the will of the other and to affirm the will of the subjects themselves. A fairly clear example can be found in the way the Chinese Communist Party discursively insists on the superiority of the Chinese 'socialist' (rather State capitalism turning fascism) form of life, while at the same time, such argumentation is accompanied by propaganda of the decline of the West, which amounts to eliminating the Other's hope of being or remaining, in an association between ceasing to be the hegemonic form of life and fully ceasing to be. This is the propaganda that the subject of State capitalism needed to listen to in order to reinforce his will and even more so when doubt is most pressing, but it is also the propaganda that liberal capitalism in the West rejects with a vital priority, because those subjects weakened by doubt in their own form of life —those who, identifying with capitalism, are dissatisfied or do not manage to maximise what they expect, because they are unemployed, have no quality of life, have difficulties with the health system, etc., find in this propaganda an expression for their own dissatisfaction. They find in this propaganda a reason for their final rejection and a way out of their crisis by converting to a new life. Those are the uprooted and the socially detached, those who stopped believing in their democratic capitalist system and who, like the subjects of the 'lying flat' movement, establish themselves as points of resistance to the universalisation of the universal. The latter are originally constituted as a resistance to a State capitalism whose economic maximisation is directly that of the State, hence the weakening of that form of life is also the weakening of the State, something which in liberal capitalism would affect corporations and private companies and thus also the sources of wealth and employment.

This is not a prescription for a particular hegemony, as Butler's point seems to be, since, after all, the debate with Laclau and Žižek was more specifically about how to enable the hegemony of a left-wing community: 'Indeed, it seems to me that one of the tasks of the present Left is precisely to see what basis of commonality there might be among existing movements, but to find such a basis without recourse to transcendental claims.'[34] I limit myself to inferring and showing the characteristics and structure of the form of life as power, which responds to the historical cases that realise it. Its structure does not imply my adherence to any form of life other than the philosophical one. That which seeks to unveil being.

Now, bringing this section to its conclusion and as a corollary, just as we have revealed how the affirmation of the being of the form of life is an affirmation of its interest (and this is reproduced at the level of the subject), let us analyze how the latter relates to universalisation. The will to power as a tendency towards universalisation is also the way in which the form of life universalizes its

---

[34] Butler, 'Competing Universalities', p. 167.

interest. Thus, the interest in the form of life is expressed as a will to power in the sense of imposing itself as a being, and, therefore, imposing itself as a universal being. If the form of life affirms its interest in being what it is, it also affirms its interest in being universal. That is, it is an affirmation of the interest in becoming universal. This is equivalent to the interest of imposing its being in an exclusive way. Therefore, if the affirmation is an interest in being, universalisation is an interest in imposing one's being on others. The form of life is affirmed and universalised, and in doing so, it identifies itself with its interest. The latter is, therefore, the principle of power as another essential dimension of the form of life. The form of life as power. And the principle of the former is identified with the interest of the latter. Where a principle is identified, it is also an interest. Power, as an imposition of being, is always driven by interest. This interest is intensified in the progress of identification. And thus, also, the greater the degree of integration, the greater the identification with it. This means that the universalisation of interest is the universalisation of the power of the form of life or the form of life as power. The subject similarly incarnates that interest, which is first and utmost self-interest —extended to the community that shares it.

Therefore, the subject is also constituted by the interest of gradually imposing on himself the being with which he identifies. This interest in imposing on himself the being of the form of life consists of willing to continue being, since being the subject of the form of life entails benefits or what the subject considers to be benefits. That is, the interest in being that form of life correlates with benefits. Ontologically, the correlative benefit of the interest is that of being, imposing his being on other subjects and disinteresting himself from those who insist on their status as a non-being, which can later be studied as marginalization and suppression. The ontological interest of the subject is that of being. The subject is interested in being, that is, in incarnating that form of life, and doing it with the greatest perfection. Those who do so, as we examine below, are those who consider themselves the elites of their form of life. It must also be said that this ontology of benefits is the basis of the desire for any material or non-material profit (i.e., status, titles, privileges, influence, etc.) by the subjects of a form of life. The concrete material or non-material profit is not possible without the ontological benefit of being the subject of a form of life. This concrete profit is in proportion to the ontological benefit. Thus, the more integrated into the form of life and the greater affirmation of his being, that is, the greater perfection in the incarnation of his form of life, the greater the concrete profits of the subjects, since greater is also their interest and expectations regarding their principle. If, for example, the principle is profit maximization, his interest is to perfectly incarnate his principle, which results in obtaining concrete profits (material and non-material, that is, economic and social status).

Chapter 4

The Will-to-Will and Will-to-Power: Spontaneity

From what has been said so far, it must be understood that the will-to-power is spontaneous, as is the will to affirm oneself in the being that one is. But this spontaneity, as we said above, is rooted in the possibility of being. And specifically, in the opposite being as possibility, that is, the form of negativity from which it emerges. This emerging is spontaneous because it originates from the will-to-be a particular being other than its opposite, making thus necessary what is merely possible. From *a phenomenological point of view*, in his being, the subject experiences himself as fleeing from something, resisting an opposing force, that force being his constitutive opposite, his form of negativity. Above all else, he wants to be, but that which he wants to be emerges as affirmation and postulated hope with respect to that which he does-not-want-to-be, that from which he flees. The slogan of the students of May '68, 'We don't know what we want, but we know what we don't want', describes the constitution of subjectivity and being, and is symptomatic of the process of transformation, which is always possible. But returning to the experience of the subject, among the multiple possibilities, what determines the affirmation of his being is the fear of a concrete possibility, of a particular being understood as a possibility or even a threat. He does not want to be that, so he opts for its opposite. But from *the transcendental level*, both are simultaneous, for the affirmation of one posits its opposite as its constant possibility in retrospect. Here, we must, therefore, note at all times the difference between the transcendental level and the phenomenological or experiential level. In politics, for example, from the experience of the organisation of one's own and common life, fear is always what puts us in a position to self-impose our being, that is to say, the form of life of a community or the conversion to another one. The presentation of the opposite, of that form of negativity and those non-subjects as phantoms, intensifies self-affirmation, which can take the form of a nationalism, a racist movement, etc. It is in this experience that our being is rooted as a permanent possibility, for in being one or its opposite, we are presented with the particular way of our being. And again, its spontaneity manifests itself in this need to flee, but it derives from an original need to give itself a being that, as said above, comes with its constitutive opposite.

So, that will-to-be is constituted by the will-to-will, and both are dimensions of the will. For the will-to-be and will-to-power are, above all, the will-to-will them. It is ultimately a will. It is as much a general will in the manner of Schelling or a will-to-live rooted in the species and nature, as it is the will-to-will this or that, the first 'will' being the one on which the emphasis is placed. A will that has more to do with submission of the self-will to Schelling's universal will (reason or understanding) if the latter is taken as the universal of a form of life for a community:

> The principle, to the extent that it comes from the ground and is dark, is the self-will of creatures which, however, to the extent that it has not yet been raised to (does not grasp) complete unity with the light (as principle of understanding), is pure craving or desire, that is, blind will. The understanding as universal will stands against this self-will of creatures, using and subordinating the latter to itself as a mere instrument.[1]

And in the second sense, more clear is the analogy with the second order volition of Harry Frankfurt, his 'to want what he wants to want';[2] that will which expresses the identification of the subject/agent with a way of being and acting so that one does not simply want to do this or that, but *wants* to want it. Thus, second-order volition makes possible, and in a certain way, requires, the first-order volition. However, without a precise intentional object, this will has itself as object. This is the will to always will something and to keep on willing. This will, prior to its relation to the will-to-be as its intentional object, is thus the condition of possibility of every will. If it were not so, the form of life and the subjects would not be beings in the process of self-foundation. There would not be any being, and there would not be transformation of being. The will-to-be and the will-to-power are spontaneous then because they are constituted by the will-to-will. And all three are but a single will in which we make this analytical-transcendental distinction. Thus, as 'will-to-will', it responds to existence or life itself but, as 'will-to-will a particular being', it already responds to identification with that way of being. That is to say, it responds to the will to determine itself in a particular being. Again, the relationship is not that of priority, for the will-

---

[1] Wilhelm Joseph Schelling, *Philosophical Investigations into the Essence of Human Freedom*, p. 32.

[2] Harry Frankfurt, 'Freedom of the Will and the Concept of a Person', *The Journal of Philosophy*, 68 (1971), 5-20 (p. 17). For a development of this analogy between Schelling and Frankfurt, see Jörg Noller, '"Will is Primal Being": Schelling Critical Voluntarism', in *The Concept of Will in German* Idealism (Berlin: De Gruyter, 2020): 'Second-order volitions are not to be understood in the sense of a general law—the Kantian moral law—but in the sense of the use of this general will, which is entirely 'interwoven' with the self-will', (p. 196).

to-be is entirely will-to-will, and if the former is *being* and the latter is *existence*, then in a form of life both are simultaneous: Being is the existence of the subject as a particular way of being and acting. Existence is always realised in a particular way of being. Now, we must examine more closely this will-to-will and its relationship to other structural features of the form of life. Besides, we must clarify in what sense this ontology can be understood as vitalism.

4.1. The Unity of the Three Aspects of the Will

The will-to-will is the possibility of persisting in willing to be and to power. This will-to-will, therefore, is what is manifested both in the affirmation of the form of life and in its power. This will is the passage from the possibility to the actualization. But it is rooted in being as a possibility of itself. This means that *being as a possibility* is already the will-to-will its being. This guarantees that there is being. For *being as a possibility* is not yet being, and yet it is always a possibility of being. As a possibility, it is always the will-to-will. It wants to persist in its will. Because the will —the first will— is in itself pure possibility. And every ontological possibility depends on the will. But this will-to-will does not end when its possibility is being realised. On the contrary, it intensifies as it is integrated into the process of self-foundation. For the process is nothing more than this sustained will. Fichte wrote: 'We are claiming that we do will (...) to continue existing, not for the sake of continued existence in itself, but for the sake of a particular state of continued existence; we do not regard continued existence as an absolute end, but as a means to some end. This is obviously confirmed by experience. All human beings desire life for the sake of something'.[3] Thus, the will as a will-to-be is in reference to a particular being, while the will-to-will is always the possibility of that being; it is existence or life. This will is manifested in the will-to-be and the will-to-power of a particular form of life. This will-to-will is the ontological reason for the spontaneity of being. As mentioned above, however, the phenomenological experience of spontaneity does not reveal this will directly but through the flight from what we do not want to be. We spontaneously identify ourselves with an image of being human, which we essentially fear in its reverse. The capitalist fears austerity, the religious fears individualistic humanism, the philosopher fears the ignorant and alienated life, the artist fears the life of the automaton without self-expression, etc. In a transcendental way, however, our spontaneity springs from the life component of the will-to-be, which supersedes life itself.

The spontaneity of the self-foundation is explained phenomenologically by the will to flee from the opposite, the non-being. This flight from non-being is,

---

[3] Johann Gottlieb Fichte, *The Foundations of Natural Right* (Cambridge: Cambridge University Press, 2000), p. 107.

at this level, the possibility of being. And that *possibility of being* is intertwined with the will-to-will —which cannot be said to be neither non-being nor being. Without it, there would be no will-to-be or will-to-power: 'Thus this particular willing is the condition of all willing; its realization (…) is the condition of all other actions and of every expression of freedom.'[4] This will-to-will and to persist in willing is constant as a 'liminal territory'. That's why there are always new possibilities of being. And that's why *being as a possibility* of oneself can also be a possibility of another being. When there is a contradiction in the foundation of being, that is, a situation of deadlock, the will pushes as a possibility of transformation. That is, the will continues willing. That is why paralysis or indetermination is only a moment of crisis and not a permanent state. Because as a permanent State it would be the end of its possibilities, and, therefore, the end of its will to persist in willing. Or what is the same, the absolute non-being, contrary to the relative non-being —being as possibility—, which is the counterpart of a determinate being or of a particular form of life.

This will-to-will is also the drive of power, for again, power is the determination of life. This will-to-will has an intentional object, because to will is always to will something. But primarily, the object is the will itself; the will becomes self-absorbed. It wills itself. And to will itself is to will to persist in willing, since that is what willing is. Hence, its object is to will itself constantly. And to will itself constantly is to keep the will active, that is, to continue willing. So, the will-to-will, by remaining active, maintains the will-to-be and the will-to-power. Or what is the same, by remaining as the will of itself, it keeps alive the will of other intentional objects. That is, the self-affirmation and self-foundation of being are ultimately driven by its self-volition, which guarantees its self-preservation. For being *as a possibility* is a will that has itself as the object of its will: 'Every will has itself (in the future) as an object. Everything that wills has self-preservation as its final end'.[5] And in willing itself, it wills to affirm its particular being and power. Without will, there is no possibility of a particular being. So, nestled within the will-to-be, this self-volition is the origin of the process. And it is where the spontaneity of the process is explained. This self-volition wills to will itself to remain as a possibility. The will-to-will as the origin of the process is what explains why the process is infinite, because the will-to-will would cease if the object, which is itself, were realised. The will to will seeks to continue willing, or what is the same, it seeks to continue having itself as an intentional object, as a possibility. And in this sense, it is the will to live in Schopenhauer's terms, for 'what the will wills is always life'.[6] For in life, the will wills itself. But

---

[4] *Ibid.*

[5] Fichte, *Foundations of Natural Right*, p. 134.

[6] Schopenhauer, *The World as Will and Representation*, p. 275.

as a particular possibility, this will-to-will is also determined in the form of negativity. Already in the form of negativity, one glimpses the being of the form of life that originates from its will-to-be. For in this form, there is already being and power. With regard to being, it has already been said that by willing itself as a possibility, it wills the affirmation of its particular being. With respect to power, as the imposition of its being upon itself, the will-to-will is manifested in the will to continue imposing itself, the will to continue winning over itself. For this is the imposition on oneself, a way of winning over oneself as the incarnation of a form of life. The subject thus experiences his identity as a constant and unlimited task. And in this sense, politics is also unlimited with respect to the identity of the community. It tends endlessly to realise an identity and a being that can never be attained. That is why it also struggles to resist or universalise irremediably and indefinitely.

It must be clear then that the will-to-will is the driving force behind the will-to-be and the will-to-power. But also that the three form an indissoluble unity in the form of life, and that is why being, even though it is the opposite of life (which I take it as the same as existence), assimilates it and takes it into its bosom. The will-to-will is thus the origin of the spontaneity of the process, and it is superseded by it. This spontaneity is fundamental to understand in what sense the form of life as a political constitution of life is at the same time necessary and free, and so is the State, which is built on the form of life. On the other hand, it is this spontaneity that explains that the imposition of the being is always a self-imposition and not an external imposition or constraint. The spontaneity and freedom with which we endow our being, our life project, is based on this will-to-will, as a possibility of possibilities, that is to say, on existence as a transcendental and impersonal immanence. On this existence, the will-to-be is the affirmation of a way of being and acting, consciousness and body, that is, principled actions. So, the origin of the form of life is not situated in the constitutive nothingness of consciousness, as Sartre would have it for the subject's life project,[7] but rather in existence itself, which is the transcendent and inherent possibility of the subject's meaningful actions in the world. And this is because existence is the absence of the affirmation of being, which is self-consciousness (as the original anthropical image) realised through actions in the world. Existence as in-itself is indeterminate, the totality of possibilities of being. It is as for-itself-in-itself that being irrupts, as politics irrupts. If we point out that by being I mean the ontological notion of the form

---

[7] Sartre, *Being and Nothingness*: 'When I constitute myself as the comprehension of a possible as my possible, I must recognize its existence at the end of my project and apprehend it as myself, awaiting me down there in the future and separated from me by a nothingness.' (p. 41).

of life that I have developed in previous sections, one could again bring up Fichte, in whose 1804's lectures (the so-call second period), I have found a very similar thought on being and life: 'The presupposed life in itself should be entirely and unconditionally in-itself; and it is intuited as such. Therefore, all being and life originates with it, and apart from it there can be nothing.'[8]

4.2. Deleuze and Life as 'Absolute Immanence'

Now, in Deleuze, one can read a notion of existence or life in terms similar to those I have just mentioned: as an 'absolute immanence' that nevertheless cannot be apprehended in reflection. This apprehension, rather, would be proper to Fichte —and also of my account— as Gaetano Rametta suggests: 'Fichte shows how without consciousness life would be impossible in its appearing, that is, how life would cease to be life at all'.[9] For Deleuze, life as pure or absolute immanence affirms itself, and the way to perceive it is by reducing the reflective process of consciousness, a consciousness liberated from the reflective self, as a sort of impersonal consciousness. Gaetano Rametta puts it like this: 'Deleuze tries to eliminate the "self" from "consciousness", in order to conceive an absolutely impersonal experience of the impersonal and indefinite becoming of life.'[10] On the other hand, the existence that I have correlated with the form of life can rarely be intuited in itself —unless in a mystic experience—, because it presupposes going beyond the being that we are, beyond our particular possibilities, even if that beyond is within ourselves as constitutive will. Life can only be apprehended in the affirmation we make of ourselves as subjects acting in the world, and thus as reflective consciousness about our being. What we necessarily get is a life that is not infinite and indeterminate becoming, Deleuze's 'pure virtuality',[11] for that would be impossible for the concreteness of our being, but a form of life in which the absolute has been denied in a particular determination. And we cannot even be conscious of that determination in its totality, only of those aspects that we actualise. But what we do grasp in each of our actions is the impersonal principle of being with which we have voluntarily and spontaneously constituted ourselves. This principle is the law of the anthropical image that constitutes our non-positional consciousness as a transcendent-immanent

---

[8] Johann Gottlieb Fichte, The Science of Knowing. *J. G. Fichte's 1804 Lectures on the Wissenschaftslehre* (New York: State University of New York Press, 2005), p. 95.

[9] Gaetano Rametta, 'Consciousness. A Comparison between Fichte and the Young Sartre', in Fichte and the Phenomenological Tradition, ed. by Violetta Waibel, Daniel Breazeale and Tom Rockmore (Berlin: De Gruyter, 2010), p. 318.

[10] Rametta, 'Consciousness. A Comparison between Fichte and the Young Sartre', p. 319.

[11] Gilles Deleuze, *Pure Immanece. Essays on a Life* (New York: Zone Books, 2001), p. 31

that incorporates existence as will-to-will. If it is not an 'absolute immanence', for we can be reflectively conscious of it through our actions —for that is why we act at all—, it does operate in an impersonal transcendental field defined by Deleuze as 'a pure stream of a-subjective consciousness, a pre-reflexive impersonal consciousness, a quality duration of consciousness without a self'.[12] So, the anthropical image is that transcendental field which the subjects of a community have in common, affirmed by their particular will-to-be; it is that shared image of being human which cannot be said to be of just one individual. Above and beyond our individuality, we are profoundly and constitutively impersonal, which underlies our communality.

This is a transcendental field, nevertheless, that, contrary to Sartre and Deleuze, is not and cannot be nothingness, life or pure will-to-will: 'a life is the immanence of immanence, absolute immanence: it is complete power, complete bliss'.[13] It must already be 'a will-to-will a particular way of being'. That is to say, a will-to-be that is the way in which life, or will-to-will, persists in itself. A non-positional consciousness is already that of a will-to-be from which any other will emerges as an intentional act and positional consciousness. What this means on a phenomenological level is that what the subject desires does not come from a will-to-will or from life itself, but from a will-to-be as an original act of willing that configures the framework of possibilities of our desires and actions. In this will-to-be, life throbs, it is true, but it is not life itself that constitutes us, which, as indeterminate and absolute becoming, could not, but that original will-to-be, contradictory to life, which, by affirming itself, determines our possibilities of thought and action.

The will-to-be a particular being is our original state, in the sense that our transcendence is constituted by our immanent act of the will as self-imposition, for as the same Deleuze says: 'Transcendence is always the product of immanence'.[14] Without this will-to-be there would be no intentionality. All our intentional acts arise from that will-to-be, which, as has been said, is the affirmation of a being as in-itself-for-itself, in which in its original consciousness lies the totality of its possible meaningful actions. All intentional acts arise from that will because we could not will something without an ultimate motivation, which constitutes the subject as a being. And that constitution cannot be life or existence in itself, for it is indeterminate, infinite openness, the nothingness to which Sartre refers and which cannot, as I have said, simply constitute our consciousness. This nothingness is, in any case, the posited possibility that determines that we necessarily have to impose on

---

[12] Deleuze, *Pure Immanece*, p. 25

[13] Deleuze, *Pure Immanece*, p. 27.

[14] Deleuze, *Pure Immanece*, p. 31.

ourselves the being, the form of life, from which all intentionality is born, which transforms arbitrariness into the necessary possibilities of the being that we have wanted to be and which we affirm with every meaningful action. The infinity and absolute becoming of life is assimilated by the will-to-be as that constant persistence in the given being, progressively intensifying its degree of realisation to the point of absolute self-identity, as we have already referred to.

Thus, only analytically can we separate the will-to-will from the will-to-be, life from the form of life, while recognising that they are not at all the same without being thereby completely distinct, and this can be illustrated by the way Deleuze once again defines immanence as the virtualities of life which on the transcendental plane are actualised by various forms: 'There is a big difference between the virtuals that define the immanence of the transcendental field and the possible forms that actualize them and transform them into something transcendent'.[15] This indicates once again that the affirmation of life, even that resounding, pure and unguarded affirmation of life of which Nietzsche was its best advocate, that 'YES',[16] cannot but be given through the particular form of life of each subject. *I affirm myself and affirm life, by affirming my form of life, which is my way of acting, being and feeling, with its constitutive principle. I affirm life as a political subject.* There is no way to affirm life as such in its immanence, for it is an in-between a form of life and death; even in the example Deleuzes provides of a novel of Dickens, he refers to 'a moment that is only that of *a* life playing with death. The life of the individual gives way to an impersonal and yet singular life that releases a pure event freed form the accidents of internal and external life, that is, from the subjectivity and objectivity of what happens'.[17] Furthermore, these virtualities, which are the possible possibilities of life, in their immanence, in their will-to-will, as non-positional consciousness, are already an affirmation of a form of life, of a way of being. They comprise a pre-ontological principle that consciousness grasps as a necessary possibility or what Sartre in *Being and Nothingness* formulates as: 'a "pre-ontological comprehension" of being which is involved in every kind of conduct belonging to "human reality" —i.e., in each of its projects'.[18] Life beyond our consciousness is just impossible virtualities, infinite multiplicity.

---

[15] Deleuze, *Pure Immanece*, p. 32.

[16] Nietzsche in *Thus Spoke Zarathustra* (Cambridge: Cambridge University Press, 2005), refers to that affirmation comprised in the Yes to life as such –pure existence-, which, nonetheless, would open the door to a new way of being human: 'Yes, for the game of creation my brothers a sacred yes-saying is required' (p. 17). And further on: 'Have you ever said Yes to one joy? Oh my friends, then you also said Yes to all pain. All things are enchained, entwined, enamored' (p. 263).

[17] Deleuze, *Pure Immanence*, p. 28.

[18] Sartre, *Being and Nothingness*, p. 17.

But this consciousness has to affirm itself as being in the world, with the body, therefore reflectively, with a behaviour that we will perform and justify.

Thus, the will, as will-to-will, is infinite, that is, a possibility of itself that wants to continue to be so, while at the same time, as will-to-be, founds itself necessarily. There is, therefore, a paradox or contradiction in this process, an inherent contradiction that, as in the entire ontology of the form of life, is generated by its dialectical structure. That is, although the will-to-be and the will-to-power are driven by the will-to-will, the first two are directed towards an object or end that is contradictory to that of the second, a contradictory movement that, nevertheless, maintains the being of the form of life, and founds it without ever ceasing to be a possibility. Thus, on the one hand, the will-to-will is the origin of the process of self-foundation as a permanent, never-fulfilled possibility. And on the other hand, the will-to-be and will-to-power are the origin of the process of necessary integration in a particular being where its possibility is progressively determined. Heidegger draws from Nietzsche's idea of power, and writes:

> Life not only exhibits the drive to maintain itself, as Darwin thinks, but also is self-assertion. The will to maintain merely clings to what is already at hand, stubbornly insists upon it, loses itself in it, and so becomes blind to its proper essence. Self-assertion, which wants to be ahead of things, to stay on top of things, is always a going back into its essence, into the origin. Self-assertion is original assertion of essence.[19]

Life or the will-to-will seeks self-preservation, but the form of life as will-to-power seeks the assertion of the original will-to-be, i.e., 'the essence' in Heidegger's terms. So, the will-to-will, willing itself as a perpetual possibility, contradicts the two respective wills of being and power that want the affirmation and imposition of a particular being. *In this unavoidable contradiction lies the break with existence as pure self-preservation without ceasing to have it as the necessary background of the particular being that constitutes us.* And if this, insofar as it determines and sets up an organised existence, can be considered to be political, as has been said above, it must be inferred that politics is in that sense opposed to existence, or rather, implies a necessary break with all those possibilities that are not the particular possibility that we have affirmed —as subjects and community.

The will-to-power wants to impose itself and, therefore, to cancel some possibilities; that is to say, to integrate and find itself. Every display of power is an

---

[19] Martin Heidegger, *Nietzsche: The Will to Power as Art*, 2 vols. (San Francisco: Harper, 1991), I, pp. 60-61.

exercise in determination. The freedom and spontaneity of the will-to-will is thus determined and bounded in the process of affirmation and imposition. And yet, such freedom and spontaneity remain indispensable in the whole process of self-foundation. In fact, it is the process of self-foundation that motivates the imposition and affirmation of the particular being of the form of life. That is why both are perpetual contingent necessities. We must bear in mind, however, that the end or aim of the form of life as being and power is always in ontological contradiction with the aim of the form of life as a possibility. This means that the imposition and universalisation of being, even if it is a spontaneous tendency of the will-to-power, is against the form of life as a perpetual possibility. To impose the being is to present it as necessary, which in turn leads to integrating one more degree in its totalization, while at the same time concealing its condition of constant mere possibility as deriving from the will-to-will. This concealing of the being of the form of life as perpetual possibility is structural of the integration process. On the phenomenological level, the subject experiences that he is given only one way of conducting himself in life at a time, although this is modified and developed at different stages of the progress. It is at this level that the subject lives his life immanently oblivious of his own transcendence. This is the *natural attitude* described by Husserl [*der natürlichen Einstellung*].[20] What was demanded of the subject yesterday, which he spontaneously imposed on himself as his authentic way of being, has today given way to other demanded behaviours, although the principle that drives them is always maintained. For example, the effect of technology is evident, as today it seems that there is no way of being human without at least owning one mobile phone, various forms of digital payment, several accounts on social media, etc., all of which rest in the certainty of digital connectivity as can be read in the contribution to a Pew Research survey: 'Hyperconnection is part of my family and friends' well-being. It is nothing that can be compared with the life my parents had. I wonder how I could have survived in that society, living before total digital connectivity existed, even when it had just started and was not spread yet'.[21]

And the same is true of other phenomena, such as education. At this stage of the process of the hegemonic capitalist form of life, it seems to the subject that there has always been compulsory secondary education; it does not seem that there can be an alternative —when, in fact, this transformation is a product of

---

[20] Edmund Husserl, *Ideas Pertaining to a Pure Phenomenology and to a Phenomenological Philosophy. First Book: General Introduction*, volume 2 of *Collected Works* (Dordrecht, The Netherlands: Kluwer Academic Publishers, 1983), §§ 27–33.

[21] Anecdote from Ana Cristina Amoroso das Neves. See Stories From Experts About the Impact of Digital Life | Pew Research Center. This is what I call rationalization and it is part of the propaganda of a form of life from the individual standpoint.

capitalism with the exodus from the countryside to the city and the need to educate and assimilate the children of the new urban proletariat—, and yet such an alternative may well be glimpsed in the future progress of the same capitalist form of life.[22] Of course, it would be a digitalised or virtual secondary education in which even the compulsory component will be revised when the mechanisation of the production chain gets supervised by artificial intelligence, and human workers become superfluous in more and more professional areas such as teachers, chemist, lawyers, doctors, etc.[23]

By this, I mean that the demand with which one is confronted and which makes one direct his own actions towards various things and subjects would lose effectiveness if it were presented as a non-urgent, non-definite demand, that is, as a demand that can be deferred, by which it is understood that it will necessarily be modified in the future. Something along the lines of 'you don't need it now because it will soon be outdated'. On the contrary, the demand of the form of life, even if it is temporary with respect to its progress of integration and totalisation, always presents itself to the subject as an immediate and urgent need which, nevertheless, enables him to continue to be who he is. It is the experience that life cannot be lived without attending to this demand, because life is NOW and the self is lived as immanent to life. This structure is summed-up in the propagandistic slogan 'Renew or Die'. The subject's being is always at stake. He feels the pressure that this last stage of progress could be his last stage, which implies a retreat into the impossibility from which he flees. For example, in the capitalist, precariousness and austerity; in the artist, the reproduction of the works of art of others; in the survivor, decadence; in the philosopher, alienation as the concealment of the self, and so on.

4.3. Is this a Vitalism?

Finally, returning to our topic, we still have to discern in what sense this onto-phenomenology can be described as a vitalism. It can be considered a vitalism

---

[22] This is not mere abstract historical progress but the progress of a particular form of life towards itself, towards its totalisation. But this would bring us to the subject of the philosophy of history, which we cannot deal with here.

[23] This is at least the take of Richard and Daniel Susskind *in The Future of Professions. How Technology Will Transform the Work of Human Experts* (Oxford: Oxford University Press, 2015): 'In relation to our current professions, we argue that the professions will undergo two parallel sets of changes. The first will be dominated by automation. Traditional ways of working will be streamlined and optimized through the application of technology. The second will be dominated by innovation. Increasingly capable systems will transform the work of professionals, giving birth to new ways of sharing practical expertise. In the long run this second future will prevail, and our professions will be dismantled incrementally' (p. 271).

in the style of Nietzsche or Schopenhauer if it is stressed the origin of the process in the will-to-will, or even in the will itself, which has no ground, for it is life itself:

> This will objectifies itself as life, as existence, in such endless succession and variety, in such different forms, all of which are accommodations to the various external conditions, and can be compared to many variations on the same theme. But if we had to convey to the beholder, for reflection and in a word, the explanation and information about their inner nature, it would be best for us to use the Sanskrit formula which occurs so often in the sacred books of the Hindus, and is called Mahavakya, i.e., the great word: 'Tat tvam asi', which means 'this living thing art thou'.[24]

And so, the whole process by which the form of life endows its being to itself is driven by the will, which expresses its freedom and spontaneity. And it expresses these latter even in its capacity as the will to determine its being, as the will-to-be and will-to-power. And yet, although this is what I also claim, we must not forget the dialectical logic of the process. That which shows that *being as a possibility* is a certain non-being. And that the will-to-will consists of being a perpetual possibility of itself. A possibility that, as a denial of the particular being, is, in turn, denied by the will-to-be and will-to-power, which affirms that particular being as a form of life or totality of certain possibilities. This process, although driven by the will, which leads to the affirmation of being through activity, is, at the same time, structurally dialectical. Thus, in the possibility, there is already the principle whose affirmation depends on the negation of itself as a possibility, which in turn it is the negation of the realised being. That is why *the process is not only voluntaristic but also dialectical and logical.* Hence, the will as such is in contradiction with itself, willing to be a perpetual possibility as well as a particular being, integrated, constituted, consolidated and finally, fully founded. And this can be completed with the meaning we gave to the will in the introduction as an affirmation of a way of being and acting, that is —and in this, we part ways with Nietzsche and Schopenhauer—, the will is the affirmation of ourselves as a form of life insofar as it is our 'in-itself-for-itself', which is how politics is introduced into the world.

---

[24] Arthur Schopenhauer, *The World as Will and Representation*, 2 vols. (New York: Dove Publications, Inc., 1969), I, p. 220.

Chapter 5

The Limits of Power

From the above, it follows that all power is power precisely because it has limits, for power is primarily the self-imposition of the form of life, and this is the disposition and determination of limits to life. Without these limits, there would be no power. The latter is thus constitutively limited. This means at least the following: 1. A form of life has no power beyond the peak of its totalisation so that its power would paradoxically come to an end if it were to reach its posited full realisation and consequent elimination of its constitutive negativity, that is, the inherent Other. 2. A form of life has no power over life as such, which continues to flow indefinitely; it has power only over itself as a being in which life takes form; the latter remains immanent. The political is always threatened by life as an uncontrollable torrent, always limited as being by the anarchic freedom of what is nothing fixed, pure becoming. For on the latter, the political always floats. We will now analyse in more detail the above-mentioned limits in reverse order.

5.1. Life as Limit

The first of the limits of power as the imposition of a form of life is that of life as openness and indeterminacy. In the affirmation of possibility as the will-to-be, we find the totalizing limits of being, which is power and politics. This includes not only what we have called being *qua* being, or actuality, but also *being as possibility* or its potentiality. However, what about that territory that is left out, that of the will-to-will and the plural possibilities of being, the possible possibilities? Is that will-to-will part of the form of life and the power it exercises? We have already seen that this will is the condition of possibility of the will-to-be and the will-to-power. And as the possibility of possibilities, life is the possibility of both the will-to-be and the will-to-power. In a word, it is the source of all forms of life, but it is also the opposite of the form of life: 'This tension consists in the fact that things are given life precisely by their opposite, by that which is other than themselves'.[1] If the latter is the will-to-be something particular, the former is the will to continue to will and never to be reduced to a particular form of being. If the former is determination, the latter is openness, freedom, spontaneity. Our research has thus led us to one of its most important

---

[1] Byung-Chul Han, *The Expulsion of the Other* (Cambridge: Polity Press, 2018), p. 10.

findings. That of the limits of the form of life, of power and politics, but at the same time dialectically that which does not cease to constitute negatively the former. It is the realm of non-being as indeterminacy. From the phenomenological point of view, it is the posited absolute that the will-to-be opposes when the subject endows himself with a particular form of life. With the latter, being is born, leaving behind the darkness and the will without an object beyond itself; leaving behind life as an absolute immanent, in the aforementioned Deleuze's notion.[2]

Now, we can only glimpse that realm; that is, we cannot discern its characteristics except in an apophatic way, as opposed to the being of the form of life. And we do so because it is important to understand the ultimate meaning of this ontological investigation. If the form of life is political, life as absolute will-to-will is apolitical. If, in the political organisation of life, the necessary possibilities of the subject are established, in life, as the realm of the indeterminate, the possible possibilities are offered. If the *necessary possibilities* refer to actions and attitudes that define the identity of the subject, the *possible possibilities* refer to the passivity and the stillness of that which has neither a defined identity nor imposed habits. If the form of life and its will-to-be impose a *discourse*, from life and its will-to-will is born the *word*, as a cancellation of discourse, for there is nothing there to justify or praise. The word is not even symbolic, for that would require a form of life in which it would make sense; the word of this dark realm of life refers to itself and not to an external framework of meaning. It is pure openness, indeterminate; it is barely a sound that is born from the entrails of life, a voice with which it affirms itself. If in the form of life arise the emotions of love and liking with which we self-realise as those subjects we want to become so perfectly, in the realm of life is found generosity, as that in which identity is dispersed, opening us to the absolute-Other through the cracks of our being. This absolute is immanent to being, but is originally posited outside as the negation of being and, therefore, what being is not.

It is the limit that delirium presents to reality. There cannot be one without the other, and indeed, power is power because it sets limits within life. That is why these two terms limit each other: life and the form of life. For this very reason, it seems essential to recognise that the being that we are, our life project and the behaviours that we take as necessary in our community, are one among many other possibilities, without saying that they are not therefore important and necessary, because without endowing ourselves with a particular way of being, we would not be able to maintain life as the original source of our will-to-be. Therefore, the form of life we have given ourselves is the way in which we preserve life; the latter, if obscure and indeterminate, generous and free, is

---

[2] Deleuze, *Pure Immanence*, p. 27.

precisely what makes us continue to want to be what we are. To eliminate the form of life in order to attain pure life is the same as eliminating life itself; to become a non-being in an inert or cataleptic state. However, it is in the original immanent life that the subject truly escapes from power. The limit to it comes precisely from those moments, raptures or delusions in which the subject evades, and is almost transfigured, suspending his being for a fleeting moment... ceasing to affirm and impose himself... And ultimately, as we shall see in the chapter on ethics, power becomes impotent in the face of the omnipotent, non-defiant openness of generosity. The latter cannot be understood without this going beyond the form of life, this going beyond self-imposed limits, without this constitutive indeterminacy, without this freedom, which is the condition for the *possibility of being*. Curiously, it is in this interstice between the political and life that Alain Badiou thinks of what he calls *politics*, the 'realm of the real', beyond the communitarian union and identity specifications of the will-to-power: 'Let us pose axiomatically that the free mobility of politics stems from the face that it touches upon the real by way of an interruption, and not by way of a gathering. That politics is an actively intervening-interpreting thought, and not the assumption of a power'.[3] Badiou's politics seems to emerge from the common ground that is life, as an event that suddenly gives meaning to individual and collective action, opening up a new way of understanding reality. It is event, undecidable, mobility, exception, non-regulation, unrepresentable, etc., and therefore requires courage, for like the generosity I have mentioned, which also requires courage, it is unguided, out of the context of meaning that constitutes its form of life: 'Whatever may be the belief that escorts it on the basis of the political, politics cannot do without courage, which we can define, at the opposite end of anxiety, as the split precipitation into the undecidable'.[4] Politics is that going beyond the particular form of life and finding a new possibility of being and acting. As an event, one could associate it, for example, with the French revolution, but bearing in mind that as a sojourn in the field of the Lacanian real —roughly what I call the will-to-will— the revolution should be constant, the impossible of endless mobility, in order not to fall into the political as the cancellation of the spontaneity of the event ('politics') and the fixation of the temporary union of individual wills in a kind of stable social relation within the form of life. For 'relationships touch upon politics only by way of its fixation. The mobility that is politics does not find its truth in the social relation. It is that which testifies to a nonrelation, to the slippage of a de-linking. This is what matters in politics, even though the

---

[3] Alain Badiou, *Can Politics be Thought?* (Durham and London: Duke University Press, 2018), p. 36.
[4] Badiou, *Can Politics be Thought?*, p. 37.

visibility of this nonrelation depends on a tightening of the conceptual screws around the relation itself'.[5] Politics in Badiou's version, as born of an unrepeatable and unrepresentable event, thus verges on the mystical and the poetic, the ground on which the political will is founded and fixed.

If philosophy can unveil the form of life as being, only mysticism and the poetic word can lead to that realm of non-being, on which, however, all that is depends. If philosophy deals with reality, mysticism deals with the delusions of the real. To glimpse this terrain, not only mysticism but also the thought of María Zambrano, the counterpart of power and the political, is indispensable. For, with her poetic reason (*razón poética*), she comes to our aid here to understand what we have left aside, what always remains unsaid, that will-to-will, that possibility of possibilities that is LIFE, and from where Badiou's event emerges. Perhaps the Spanish philosopher is right, and it is only poetry that is able to express that life beyond being and beyond the form of life we have imposed on ourselves, with its political determination (a beyond that is nonetheless constitutive of it). She draws a comparison between philosophy and poetry. While philosophy strives to reveal being, poetry shows life as non-being, or the possibility of being. For in that background of life, being vanishes in its exclusivity. She wrote: 'there is something in man that is neither reason, nor being, nor unity, nor truth —that reason, that being, that unity, that truth. But it was not easy to prove it, nor was it wanted to, because poetry was not born in polemics, and its generous presence was never asserted polemically. It did not arise in the face of anything'.[6] Poetry is thus a mode of generosity, which consists in pure openness. A poetry that should be associated with mysticism, perhaps a mystical poetry, which expresses that creative nothingness as a possibility of possibilities; a poetry in which the individual, beyond his form of life, temporarily converted into a non-subject, approaches that impossible nothingness, experiences it perhaps as an impossible but constitutive absence, while remaining rocked in that indeterminate attitude that Zambrano identifies with love, and which I, as I will show later, prefer to call generosity; the generosity of ceasing to impose one self's being: 'The poetry of St. John of the Cross, where at the same time as the whole human being the creatures shine —nature, in truth, as a new-born child— shows this fecundity of approaching, impossible in principle, to the nothingness that is made in the

---

[5] *Ibid.*

[6] María Zambrano, *Filosofía y poesía* (México D. F.: Fondo de Cultura Económica, 2005), p. 16: 'hay algo en el hombre que no es razón, ni ser, ni unidad, ni verdad —esa razón, ese ser, esa unidad, esa verdad—. Mas no era fácil demostrarlo, ni se quiso, porque la poesía no nació en la polémica, y su generosa presencia jamás se afirmó polémicamente. No surgió frente a nada'. Translation in English is mine.

sole way of love'.[7] The poetic word, according to Zambrano, is that which, contrary to discursive reason, which is always opposed to something and is therefore born to justify or praise as well as to reject and denigrate, springs from the multiplicity of life beyond the form of life in which the multiple and indeterminate is accommodated as a unity. For she wrote: 'Poetry pursued, meanwhile, the disdained multiplicity, the scorned heterogeneity'.[8] If being is unity and is expressed in rational discourse, what is not or is indeterminate is expressed through the poetic word; the latter would be the one that would show reality in its incessant becoming, as Nietzsche already conceived it.[9]

That real is the one that is beyond the reality that constitutes for the subjects their form of life, that is why it can rightly be called 'delirium', a delirium that regarding life as absolute immanence implies a certain death of the being of the subject: 'the creature, helpless, delirious on the edge of life and death. Delirium of the life that springs up amidst death. Life always appears delirious, as if it were itself the delirium of a starting heart'.[10] In delirium, the poetic word captures the real in its multiple unrealised possibilities. Hence, Zambrano says that the poet aspires, as does every subject in his form of life, and especially the philosopher in his philosophical form of life, to totality. But in the poet, this totality is the final realisation of all the possibilities, and not of just one form of life but of each and every one of them, those already actualised in the world and those not yet conceived. This is something that reminds us of the aspiration to realise an ideal of humanity, as in Fichte and Krause.[11] The poet would thus be that priest of humanity who announces its possibilities: 'the poet's "whole" is quite different, for it is not the whole as a horizon, nor as a

---

[7] María Zambrano, *Notas para un método* (Madrid: Mondadori, 1989), p. 17: 'La poesía de San Juan de la Cruz, donde al par que el ser humano entero resplandecen las criaturas – la naturaleza, en verdad, como recién nacida-, da muestra de esta fecundidad del aproximarse, imposible en principio, a la nada que se hace en la sola vía del amor'. Translation in English is mine.

[8] Zambrano, *Filosofía y poesía*, p. 13: 'La poesía perseguía, entre tanto, la multiplicidad desdeñada, la menospreciada heterogeneidad.' Translation in English is mine.

[9] Sarah Kofman, *Nietzsche et la Métaphore* (Paris: Galilée, 1983).

[10] María Zambrano, *El sueño creador* (Zamora, Veracruz: Universidad Veracruzana, 1965), p. 108: 'La criatura, desamparada, delira en el filo de la vida y de la muerte. Delirio de la vida que brota entre la muerte. La vida aparece siempre delirando; como si ella misma fuese el delirio de un corazón inicial'. Translation in English is mine.

[11] Karl Christian Friedrich Krause, *Das Urbild des Menscheit* (Göttingen: Dieterichschen Buchhandlung, 1851); Karl Christian Friedrich Krause, *The Ideal of Humanity and the Universal Federation*, edited by W. Hastie (Edinburgh: T&T Clark, 1900).

beginning; but, in any case, a "whole" a posteriori, which will only be so when each thing has already reached its fullness'.[12]

In the sense indicated, then, the poetic would be the opposite of the political, at least as long as we understand the poetic with Zambrano, as that approach to expressing life in its indeterminate multiplicity. That is to say, beyond being, we cannot but contemplate and embrace the life that makes it possible as the will-to-will, perhaps through a rare event of generosity and courage that is hardly thinkable. Again, that beyond is always within being, for life is its constitutive absolute opposite. And if the imposed being of the form of life can oppose life as such, power can oppose 'love', understood as generosity and openness. All power, then, is born of life and opposes it, confronts it by determining itself. Without the original generosity, power cannot be understood, and without non-being, being cannot be grasped, for they mutually express their constitutive negativity. Any reduction of the one to the other or the other to the one is simplistic and destructive, as I hope the following pages will show.

5.2. The Other as Limit

The second limit is inherent to the process of universalisation itself, and in particular to the necessary exclusion of the forms of negativity to which it gives rise. In this exclusion, the form of life not only fails to become self-founding, but by making its negativity disappear, it also limits its existence. It should be added that universalisation, as assimilation of the negated Other, gives rise, although to a greater integration and progressive self-foundation of the self that one wants to be, at the same time, to the cause of its own destruction, for to eliminate the form of negativity is to eliminate the form of life. To suppress negativity is to eliminate oneself, since it also constitutes the subject. This intuition of the dialectic of being and the Other as the constitutive violence of the will-to-power is the topic of one of Byung-Chul Han's recent books, which expresses it in these words in relation to the hegemony of contemporary capitalist life: 'the expulsion of the Other sets in motion an entirely different process of destruction, namely that of self-destruction. In general, the dialectic of violence applies: a system that rejects the negativity of the Other develops self-destructive traits.'[13] This seems to be the price paid for the success of universalisation and the hegemony of a single identity. So, this ontological tendency announces to us a similar aspect of the form of life as power. Its

---

[12] Zambrano, *Filosofía y poesía*, p. 16: 'El "todo" del poeta es bien diferente, pues no es el todo como horizonte, ni como principio; sino en todo caso un "todo" a posteriori, que sólo lo será cuando ya cada cosa haya llegado su plenitud'. Translation in English is mine.

[13] Byung-Chul Han, *The Expulsion of the Other. Society, Perception and Communication Today* (London: Polity Press, 2018), p. 9.

possibility of being is constitutive, and as such is the negation of its actualisation. But in addition, phenomenologically, every form of life is born of its opposite, as it finds its possibility of being in flight, in separation; a separation that is never consummated but is itself constitutive. Thus, he who seeks to survive flees from death, and he who seeks to maximise flees from austerity or scarcity, and yet death and scarcity cannot but exert their presence from their constitutive absence as negativity.

For the same reason, in its dialectic, in order to be itself, the self requires that from which it flees, that negativity that reminds it that it is who it is, as someone particular and different. When the self has succeeded in throwing overboard all that is different, it ceases to be who it is. In the opposite is our possibility of being and of continuing to be. The will-to-power that drives the form of life towards universality also drives it towards its own future self-destruction, the one in which its being is completely founded by itself, without the need for justification or struggles, without fissures or differences: it is the moment of the consolidation of being together with the loss of the possibility of continuing to be who one is. The approach to this culminating moment of its totalisation could be experienced as something similar to what Byung-Chul Han calls depression: 'The pathological sign of our times is not repression but depression. Destructive pressure comes not from the Other but from within'.[14] The consolidation of being in its present selfhood could bring about a depression that announces self-destruction precisely by this elimination of constitutive absence: one begins to be purely and inexorably present to oneself, but without motivation to continue being. What would be the state, meaning and being of philosophy without the constitutive shadow of one's own ignorance? For the same reason, the universalisation of the universal leads to the consolidation of a being in announced implosion, a being that has denied itself the meaning and the will to continue being.

So, can the being ever completely eliminate the Other? Can the form of life rid itself of its constitutive negativity? This ultimate undoing as a limit is always posited but never achieved. For to reach it would be the real end of the form of life and its subjects, who not only would not have a motivating negativity, but the negation of its unitary constitution would also deny life as that possibility of possibilities in whose contradictory relation lies the possibility of the form of life, the being of the subjects. By this, I mean to emphasise that the phenomenon of self-destruction referred to by Byung-Chul Han is a characteristic of the process towards self-foundation and not of the limit as such. It is not the self-destruction of the form of life but a totalising process that intensifies the more the subject becomes integrated into himself, mediated by the form of life as

---

14 *Ibid.*

totalising totality. So, it must be understood that this realisation of the subject's self already implies both contrary movements: on the one hand, the movement towards the perfect incarnation of his image of being human, and on the other hand, the movement towards the elimination of any opposing image with its consequent self-destruction. In a way, self-realisation is self-destruction, insofar as it implies consuming one's own possibilities of continuing to be. When there is no more negativity, and therefore no more possibility, there is no more motivation or hope of realisation. The Other is thus constitutive of our subjectivity in various ways. But for this, we must first discern what we mean by the Other.

The Other, as we have already said, can be the Other of our own community, and in that case, it is a relative-Other, with whom we identify and share the same project. This Other is always already in oneself, we can only recognise him insofar as he is like us, in his way of being (his essential principle), acting and feeling. It is the type of subject with whom we have the experience of truly sharing a world of our own. And so, we say that with these co-subjects, we can really be who we are. It does not seem to be this Other, which is only with respect to me but not with respect to the community, the Other that Byung-Chul Han refers to. On the other hand, there is the Other that we have called the absolute-Other, who is alien to the community itself and thus to the subject. This Other exhibits a behaviour that we find unacceptable, undesirable, unrealisable. At the same time, he is driven in life by a principle with which we do not agree, and which we can only reject. In a blunt example, it is the type of subject that, for a fifteenth-century Amerindian tribe the 'conquistadores' would represent, and vice versa. But it is also the subject whom we cannot understand and whose actions shock us, whom we cannot treat as a normal way of behaving. Simply put, someone who has self-imposed the capitalist principle can never understand a subject who does not want to maximise and accumulate, who gives rather than acquires or who is happy and laughs like Socrates because he did not need any of the many items offered to him in an Athenian marketplace.[15] The reaction of a well-integrated capitalist would be something like this: 'no way, you must need something from here, have you seen this precious new acquisition...?' In the recognition of this Other as a possible possibility one approaches the recognition of the indeterminacy of life, which is the true inherent absolute.

For all this, the inevitable question, which hangs over us like a sword of Damocles, is whether there is, as I have said, any solution to the self-destructive

---

[15] Diogenes Laertius, *Lives of the Eminent Philosophers*, ed. by James Miller (New York: Oxford University Press, 2018), book 2 'Socrates', p. 74.

process of the self in its self-realisation. In Levinas's line of argument,[16] Byung-Chul Han seems to propose a turn towards this excluded Other, different with respect to the self, diametrically opposed, and thus an absolute-Other, for even their ways of conceiving and experiencing time are opposed:

> What is needed today is a temporal revolution that ushers in a completely different time; we must rediscover the time of the Other. Today's temporal crisis is not acceleration, but rather the totalization of the time of the self. The time of the Other eludes the logic of increase based on performance and efficiency, which creates a pressure to accelerate. The neoliberal politics of time does away with the time of the Other, which it considers an unproductive time (…) Unlike the time of the self, which isolates and separates us, the time of the Other creates a community. It is therefore a good time.[17]

Here the totalisation of the self is identified exclusively with neoliberal society, which from the ontology of forms of life seems rather an error of perspective, since all forms of life in their universalisation pursue such totalisation, albeit with different characteristics and consequences. In any case, this shift requires not so much a reduction of the self to the Other, but a reconciliation, in which both recognise and welcome each other in a peaceful and civilised coexistence, by which he means, in an enlightened sense, a combination of reason, friendship and beauty, which would be summed up in a politics of hospitality: 'Hospitality is the highest expression of a universal reason that has come into its own. Reason does not exercise any homogenizing power. Its friendliness enables it to acknowledge the Other in their otherness and welcome them. Friendliness means freedom (…). Hospitality promises reconciliation. Its aesthetic manifestation is beauty'.[18] And further down, he presents the politics of hospitality that connects with the state of civilisation of a society mediated by a universal reason: 'The politics of beauty is the politics of hospitality. Xenophobia is hatred, and ugly. It is an expression of a lack of universal reason, a sign that society is still in an unreconciled state. How civilized a society is can be judged by its hospitality in particular, indeed its friendliness. Reconciliation means friendliness'.[19]

---

[16] Levinas, Emmanuel, *Totality and Infinity: An Essay on Exteriority* (London, Boston, The Hague: Martinus Nijhoff Publishers, 1979).

[17] Byung-Chul Han, *The Expulsion of the Other*, p. 66.

[18] Han, *The Expulsion of the Other*, p 19.

[19] Han, *The Expulsion of the Other*, pp. 19-20.

While I have to agree with the Korean-German author's identification of the process of self-destruction of the subject and the social issue of the splitting and elimination of the Other, I cannot agree with his solution, which is in clear dissonance with the understanding of the process as necessary. If one understands as necessary the tendency of the subject to realise himself as an incarnation of his form of life, and bearing in mind that this realisation implies the negation and assimilation of the Other, and fundamentally the constitutive Other, one cannot but agree that the process is irreversible and that reconciliation with the Other is at odds with the realisation of the self. In this process, realisation and self-destruction go hand in hand, as in life and death, only the one who lives is dying. And this is not only applicable to the hegemonic form of life, to that which has become most universalised, but to all forms of life, since they all tend towards universalisation and self-foundation; that is to say, towards being the foundation of themselves, beyond their negative possibility. In this way, the subject that is driven by the principle of economic maximisation seeks indefinitely to get rid of its constitutive negativity and, therefore, seeks, unsuccessfully, to stop experiencing austerity and scarcity, which never happens. There will never come a time when this will no longer be experienced, because then, the subject would equally and instantly cease to want to maximise, and therefore, as a maximising subject, would cease to be. One maximises because one flees from scarcity, and scarcity is constantly experienced as constitutive of one's self-imposed being.

Every form of life that is different, every community that is not one's own, is experienced by this negation of one's own way of being and acting as something to flee from in order to continue being. As Charles Taylor wrote regarding the threat from the Other: 'There it is not only our security that is threatened; it is also our sense of our own integrity and goodness. To see this questioned is profoundly unsettling, ultimately threatening our ability to act'.[20] The solution for this cannot be reconciliation with the absolute-Other through hospitality. In truth, there is no solution, there is only the acceptance that this universal hospitality of the one with the Other will never be possible, never this reconciliation of real opposites. Not only has this never been possible in the history of humanity, but it is also ontologically inconsistent with the structures of the process of subjectification within a community: 'Every individual is to a great extent familiar with all the thoughts, emotions, and activities of the community. The uniformity of behavior is similar to that expected among ourselves of a member of a social "set". A person who does not conform to the

---

[20] Charles Taylor, *Modern Social Imaginaries* (London and Durham: Duke University Press, 2004), p. 182.

habits of thought and actions of his "set" loses standing and must leave.'[21] The moments in which there has been apparent reconciliation and universal peace between different peoples and forms of life, such as the so-called *Pax Americana* —the Roman peace would also be an example— are moments of mere universalisation of a universal-particular, which has thus assimilated the other forms of life, turning the absolute-Other into itself, in a paradoxical flight towards its own self-destruction. And in the process of self-affirmation, this progressive assimilation is as much a rampant negation of everything that is not oneself, for in contrast to what Byung-Chul Han suggests[22] drawing from Hegel, assimilation through the mediation of the form of life is essentially negation of the Other, not integration and reconciliation. For the Other becomes a 'We' when he identifies with our principles, habits, feelings and values. It is the voluntary acceptance of the denial of his being. Otherwise, any change in the life of the Other, if it must be a radical change of how they behave, but without the mediation that all conversion implies —rejection of the previous way of being and affirmation of a new one— is only done by the force of naked power. As Boas put it,

> Only when a new culture, a change of religion or of economic life is imposed by force, as was done by the Inca, or as happened in the early extension of Christianity and of Mohammedanism, and again in some regions during the forcible extermination of Protestantism, or as is happening now in Russia [he refers to the soviets' transformations of Russia towards a socialist state in the 1920s] in its economic readjustment, may one group succeed in the attempt to impose radical changes in culture.[23]

This radical change, however, can only refer to behaviour imposed and reproduced but without subjective identification, i.e., carried out in bad faith, or in contradiction to one's own way of being and acting. It is a similar understanding of the relationship of assimilation-resistance between different forms of life that leads Fichte to interpret the Roman conquest of Germania in the following way:

---

[21] Franz Boas, *Anthropology and Modern Life* (New York: Norton & Company, 1962), pp. 154-55.
[22] Buyng-Chul han wrote: 'Self-affirmation does not need to go along with the repression or negation of the other. It all depends on the structure of mediation. In the case of intense mediation, self-affirmation is not negating or excluding, but integrating'. In *What is Power?* (Cambridge: Polity Press, 2019), p. 51.
[23] Boas, *Anthropology and Modern Life,* p. 163.

Freedom meant to them that they remained Germans [*Deutsche*], that they continued to decide their affairs independently and originally, in keeping with their own spirit, and, likewise in keeping with their spirit, that they continued to move forward in their development, and that they passed on this independence to their posterity. Slavery was the name they gave to all those blessings that the Romans offered them, because by accepting these they could not but become something other than Germans; they would have to become half-Romans.[24]

Now, as we have said above, there is the temporary glimpse of the Other in oneself as an equally true and real possibility through the attitude of generosity. With this latter attitude, approaching the plurality of equally possible possibilities, renouncing the exclusivity of one with which we identify ourselves, we would reach a poetic vision of life in its creative nothingness. This would be, as I say, an attitude not so much of reconciliation and hospitality, for this is already political, and, therefore, self-imposition, but of an almost beatific experience of indeterminacy, perhaps Schopenhauer's tearing of the veil of Maya or Miguel de Molinos' mystical union. The political thus becomes a mystical experience of the Other.

---

[24] Johann Gottlieb Fichte, *Addresses to the German Nation* (Cambridge: Cambridge University Press, 2009), p. 109.

Conclusion: Power, State and Ethics

Our task here has been to emphasize the importance of the will as the source of the constitutive process of becoming who one is, one's power. There would be no propaganda or ideology without, first, the will to impose the possibility of being, and, second, without the will to impose the necessity of that being. The will is the origin and the driving force of the process. The will-to-be as a possibility originates in the will-to-will. That is to say, the subject wills to be a particular being and persevere in it because he wills to continue willing. To stop willing is to stop being. It is the will that, in its constant cycle, originates and maintains the will-to-be. In the passage from one to the other, being emerges as a possibility, which is still not being. At that moment, the will of the form of life already appears. But not yet the form of life as a necessary being. Propaganda is thus a moment that presupposes the will-to-be that being as a possibility. This original process is sustained throughout the integration of the subject in the form of life. For, as long as there is integration, there is the possibility of being and of persevering in it. But, this process is originated in the subject's will (or of the want-to-be-subject).

The consequence that can be extracted from it is that the process is voluntary. This means that it is free and spontaneous. But not necessarily rational in its beginnings (the rationality of the process has to do with the structure of all forms of life). It is free and spontaneous because the will is free and spontaneous. It is the self-determination of the will-to-be, because to continue willing, one has to give oneself a particular being. The perpetuation of willing is carried out through being. This paradoxically presents a being that wills to continue willing and a will that wills to be a particular being. The latter guarantees the former, as dimensions of one and the same will. The subject who imposes on himself the possibility of being gives himself the possibility of continuing to will. Self-imposition is the work of the will-to-power. And this will has only one drive. Its drive is the will-to-will, which, through being, continues to will. The subject, therefore, freely and spontaneously imposes on himself that being which presents itself as a possibility and not that being which presents itself as a mere necessity. Impositions as mere top-down impositions are only self-imposed when one experiences and understands that in them, there is a possibility for the subject's own being. Structurally, the being that one gives oneself is the being with which one identifies in its principle and interest, but that identification depends on the experience of the being as a possibility for the subject's own existence. And that possibility consists of willing to continue willing once the will-to-be has been made concrete. The subject gives himself the being that is presented to him as that possibility, namely, his form of life.

The form of life has been insistently disassociated with the terms culture, society or State, for as an ontological unit, it is, in any case, the foundation of what can be taken as the culture of a group, and only through processes of universalisation and hegemony can a form of life be the cultural foundation of a society and a State, becoming institutionalised as the ideology of both. It could be understood that the Heideggerian Dasein, as an ontological structure with respect to the human being, would be equivalent to the form of life with respect to the culture of a community and of each of its subjects. Having made this clarification, I think it necessary in this conclusion to explore briefly the consequences of this relation between the form of life and the State, warning, however, that I do not try in the following section to establish a systematic thought on the constitution of the State, but only to point out how the form of life in its notion of ontological unit and source of empirical power plays an essential role in this constitution.

Power and State

Throughout the pages of this book, it has been assumed that a form of life as a will-to-be-and-power comes to be identified with the State only through its institutionalisation by a governmental regime. Let us analyse this assertion through its implications.

The first consequence of this statement is that not all forms of life end up being identified with a State. On the contrary, only that which is recognised as the national form of life (or supranational in the case of federations or unions of States) does. This does not seem to show too much difficulty of acceptance. Once the form of life has been identified with the State, it is called national culture (its ideology). But by the same token, it is understood that there are forms of life that are not national and yet do not necessarily die out when one of them becomes the only form identified with the State. Here, 'State-identified' means that the State recognises itself and is recognised by other similar States for such a way of being and acting. But multiple questions arise; for example, what do I mean by nation? The nation would be, according to the above concepts, the community of subjects who identify with the national form of life and share it from their centre of subjectivity. They are that form of life in a way that is singularised by individual experience. We have already seen that in a society, there is rarely only one community and, therefore, only one form of life. On the contrary, what is more likely, especially in modern times, is that in a society, defined as a collection of individuals within the geographical and political boundaries of a State, one finds diverse ways of being and acting, i.e., behaviours directed by diverse ontological principles, but also diverse leaders and followers, in a word, diverse communities. And recognising this is important. Not all individuals in society constitute a single community under one State.

This begs the question, what exactly is a State from this ontological perspective? From the foundations laid out in this book, one can answer that the State is the combination of a form of life and a governmental regime. This is also inferred from the definition of nation as the community that shares a particular form of life under the auspices of the State. Thus, the State is the regime and the nation. This implies that without a form of life, there is no State, although the form of life does not need the State to exist. The State receives its power from the form of life that galvanises it. Primitive communities and many other potential or actual communities exist without constituting a State, for example, the Aeta tribe, the religious community of the Cathars in the twelfth century, the Hansenist league of the seventeenth century, the Mennonites of the nineteenth century, the Hippie community of the 1960s, the white supremacists of today, and so on. This requires either that the community establishes a government in which they recognise themselves or that the government imposes its form of life officially. The State, therefore, cannot be said to exist apart from its essential constituents. So, the State is a plus, an absence without which the constituents could not combine for the benefit of both. Government and the form of life combine to constitute a State. But what is the need to constitute a State?

On the one hand, a regime without a form of life cannot exist. The regime needs to impose a certain form of life, so that it cannot rule without a community on which to impose this form of life, which in itself implies a political organisation of life oriented by an image of being human. The laws, decrees, subsidies and plans of a government presuppose what is understood to be the desirable and praiseworthy form of life for its nation. Libertarian political thought, today, has insisted on modern States being aseptic and not promoting any particular form of life as a conception of the good life. To illustrate that, when Joseff Pieper asked Carl Schmitt 'why *The Concept of the Political* did not speak at all of the b*onum commune.* Schmitt replied, "Anyone who speaks of the b*onum commune* is intent on deception"'.[1] And Garret Robinson, commentting on this, asserts that 'most political thought today shares Schmitt's dismissal of the fundamental nature of the pursuit of the common good in political life'. For example, Fichte based the law of the State on its individual members —as it does the American Constitution founding the

---

[1] Garrett Robinson, 'The Common Good Before the Modern State', *The Regensburg Forum*, https://regensburgforum.com/2019/09/02/the-common-good-before-the-modern-State/#_ftn1 [accessed 28 October 2023].

republic on popular sovereignty—,[2] so that the State had the function of enabling the political and legal conditions for every subject to lead the life he or she wanted; in the Fichtean sense, 'this means that the freedom the rational State strives to realise for its citizens is different in kind from the freedom that characterizes the (Kantian) moral subject: political philosophy aims to promote personal, or "formal", freedom —the ability to act according to one's freely chosen ends, unhindered by the interference of others'.[3] In this sense, the State protects individual rights that are natural only as 'they are necessary if human beings are to realize their true "nature" as free and rational individuals'.[4] That function of the modern (rational) State, as Weber already pointed out,[5] is based on its monopoly of the legitimate use of physical force or what Fichte calls 'the right of coercion'.

I realise that I need to specify what exactly I call modern State, as this is often associated, as Charles Tilly does, [6] with the 'pattern which emerged in Europe in the period 1100 to 1600'.[7] But I am going to refer in particular to the liberal version of the modern State, that which can be identified roughly with Lockean political theory, the American constitution and republic, and the European liberal welfare States after the French Revolution. So, now that we have a rough definition, is it true that liberal versions of the modern State are aseptic and neutral in terms of promoting a form of life? For example, John Gray defines the liberal State as *limited State* against Nozik's more radical notion of *minimal State*: 'Most liberals, and all the classical liberals, acknowledge that the liberal State may have a range of service functions, going beyond rights. Protection and the upholding of justice and for this reason are not advocates of the

---

[2] Charles Taylor, *Modern Social Imaginaries* (Durham and London: Duke University Press, 2004): 'a constitution that places the new republic squarely within die modern moral order: as the will of a people that had no need of some preexisting law to act as a people but could see itself as the source of law.' (p. 111)

[3] Frederick Neuhouser (ed.), 'Introduction' to Fichte, *Foundations of Natural Right*, p. xxv.

[4] Frederick Neuhouser (ed.), 'Introduction' to Fichte, *Foundations of Natural Right*, p. viii. For Fichte, therefore, the freedom that the State makes possible and protects is the means for the development of the human being in his true nature, which implies a particular conception of the nature of the human being as a free and rational being, as well as a humanistic ultimate goal of maximising the benefits of such development for the collectivity of the subjects as humanity.

[5] Markus Jachtenfuchs, 'The monopoly of legitimate force: denationalization, or business as usual?' In *The Transformation of the State*, ed. by Stephan Leibfried and Michael Zurn (Cambridge: Cambridge University Press, 2005), p. 37.

[6] Charles Tilly, *Coercion, Capital and European State AD 990-1990* (Oxford: Basil Blackwell, 1990), p. 181.

[7] Joseph R. Strayer, *On the Medieval Origins of the Modern State* (Princeton: Princepton University Press, 1970), p. 12.

minimum State but rather of limited government'.[8] Drawing on Gray's quotation, does not the very definition of the State as an enabler of individual freedoms and rights as well as justice presuppose a conception of a good life (freedom to pursue one's own ends) and a form of life in the making? Is not the ultimate realisation of the individual who thinks of himself as free to the same extent that he recognises the freedom of others in his community a particular conception of what it is to be human, or rather a particular anthropical image? Is not this free self-realization of the self-conscious individuals, in the Fichtean Theory of the liberal, modern State, founded in the rational necessity of private property as 'exclusive sphere of activity within which they are free to carry out ends that are entirely their own'? Fichte himself, in establishing the correlation between law and the self-consciousness of individuals, seems to suggest that 'politics plays a deeper, formative role in constituting individuals' self-conceptions —that is, in bringing them to think of themselves as free persons who, simply by virtue of their ability to determine their own practical ends, are deserving of a set of rights identical to those of every other person'.[9] In his theory of the State, the State even has the responsibility to regulate the economy in order to facilitate the employment of individuals[10] as well as to distribute wealth in order to avoid their poverty.[11]

All these elements indicate that the political community must be governed by a certain principle that organises and constitutes the life of its members. I do not intend to go into this question in detail now; I will only say that it must be understood that when we talk about the form of life, we are talking about an ideology, as I have hinted throughout this book. Every form of life is an ideology insofar as it is a necessary realisation in praxis of certain possibilities intrinsic to an anthropical image. And every ideology we have said is a set or series of political actions, in the sense of actions with which we impose an organisation on life. The State is the institutionalization of that ideology, so the modern State institutionalizes a particular ideology or form of life, one that lies in the principle of maximising individual benefits (i.e., pleasures, abilities, material and spiritual goods, etc.), which are related to private ends.

In the same vein, Taylor, referring to the liberty —as personal independence— that the US constitution promoted with respect to the previous monarchical and authoritarian government, says that it was not only a negation of the latter but that 'it carried its own moral ideals',[12] which, according to Appleby, translated

---

[8] John Gray, *Liberalism* (Minneapolis: University of Minnesota Press, 2003), pp. 70-71.
[9] Frederick Neuhouser (ed.), 'Introduction' to Fichte, *Foundations of Natural Right*, p. xxvii.
[10] Fichte, *Foundations of Natural Right*, §18, III-IV, §11, IV-V; §19, II.
[11] Fichte, *Foundations of Natural Right*, §18, III-V.
[12] Charles Taylor, *Modern Social Imaginaries*, p. 149.

into a conception of the human being, that of, 'the man who developed inner resources, acted independently, lived virtuously, and bent his behaviour to his personal goals'.[13] This is the type of humanist subject who will concentrate on the individual maximisation of those resources and the pursuit of his private goals. Based on it, the capitalist subject will narrow these goals to profit and economic status, for 'the new kind of highly interested economic activity is seen as the cornerstone of a new ethic'.[14] Its anthropical image is incarnated by the new role model: 'the successful entrepreneur-turned-benefactor'.[15] Subsequent governments from its constitution will implement the form of life of liberal capitalism in the US as shaping the main national community[16] by bringing economic success to the forefront, a sign of salvation characteristic of Protestantism (and in particular Pietism) spread across the US in the early nineteenth century,[17] for, in Taylor words, '*commerce and entrepreneurship were not divisive, but rather redounded to the good of all and could be the basis of unity for a people* who were energetic, disciplined, and self-reliant. It was this kind of drive to progress that was making America great, free, and equal. Personal independence becomes part of *a new model of American patriotism, which has remained alive and powerful today.*'[18] What I want to point out is how the State *velis nolis*, with its governmental structure, its constitution, its laws and policies, imposes a conception or image of the human being. This relation between politics and the type of subject was already upheld by Aristotle in his *Politics*[19], and this is what McGuigan points out with respect to the neoliberal policies of Ronald Reagan and especially Margaret Thatcher in whose 'description of her own politics in 1981 (...) she remarked that the method is economic but the object is to change the soul'.[20]

---

[13] Quoted in Charles Taylor, *Modern Social Imaginaries*, p. 149.

[14] Taylor, *Modern Social Imaginaries*, pp. 151.

[15] Taylor, *Modern Social Imaginaries*, pp. 151.

[16] I say the main national community because, as Taylor realises, many other communities were left out of this society driven by the entrepreneurial impulse of the capitalist form of life.

[17] Taylor, *Modern Social Imaginaries*: 'But personal independence was not just a moral ideal for individual lives; it also related the agent to society. This reference back to society partly consisted in the fact that self-disciplined, honest, imaginative, entrepreneurial people were seen as the cornerstone of the new society, which combined order and progress. They were its chief benefactors, at once setting its moral tone and conferring the immense benefits of economic progress'. (p. 150).

[18] Taylor, *Modern Social Imaginaries*, pp. 150-51. Italics are mine.

[19] Aristotle, *Politics*. Volume 2, ed. by Jonathan Barnes (Princeton, New Jersey: Princeton University Press, 1995), 1275b1, p. 4344.

[20] Jim McGuigan, 'The Neoliberal Self'. *Culture Unbound* 6:1 (2014), pp. 223-240 (p. 224).

After these definitions, one might still ask whether it is true that current modern States do not impose a form of life, i.e., an ideology and a certain organisation on the lives of their subjects, in some cases mediated by the will of the subjects themselves and in others against their will. For, 'as Tom Mertes writes in his article "Grass-Roots Globalism", "the modern state —born as a counter-revolutionary, absolutist response to Renaissance humanism, boosted with the toxic ideology of an exclusionary, homogenizing nationalism— has always been a tool for repression, even when posing as the champion of anti-colonial liberation"'.[21] This clashes head-on with Schmitt's refusal to understand the modern State as imposing a sort of *bonum commune* or what I have called an ontological principle. By current modern State, I am thinking of Western States, such as European, American, but also current Asian States like Japan, South Korea, Singapore, Australia, etc. Modern States do not promote religious, intellectual, artistic, decadent, mercantilist, collective forms of life, but can it be said that they do not promote through their governments the profit-maximising forms of life of individuals? Are certain activities, such as private sector business, not promoted with subsidies to the detriment of others? Are consumption and products in certain areas not incentivised by tax reductions? Isn't the propaganda of consumption and wealth accumulation facilitated in the mass media and encouraged by State programs? Isn't an educational curriculum programmed to prepare students with business, commercial skills and strategies with which to compete in the labour market? According to the above discussion, it seems to be the case that the current Modern States promote a capitalist form of life. It was certainly Margaret Thatcher's intention with regard to the neo-liberal development of this form. In that sense, modern States in their liberal version may be linked indissolubly to the universalization of the liberal capitalist subject and community, with his individual maximization of economic profit within the public sphere of the society, or what, adding the element of 'self-governing polity', Taylor calls 'the modern imaginary', [22] but I claim that the self-governing issue refers only to the community that identify with the anthropical image promoted by the State and not those other communities that are left over as non-subjects, as he himself admits that 'the crucial thing about America's development is that these people who couldn't make it to the celebratory family portrait of the enterprising never could find or erect the cultural space to unite around an alternative vision of the republic'.[23] Suffice this as a reflection on the matter for now.

---

[21] David S. D'Amato, 'Understanding the Modern State', *Libertarianism.org* https://www.libertarianism.org/columns/understanding-modern-state [accessed 28 October 2023]
[22] Taylor, *Modern Social Imaginaries*, p. 152.
[23] *Ibid.*

On the other hand, if a regime needs a form of life to exist, the latter needs the former to affirm and universalise itself since, as was shown, every form of life tends towards universalisation. Those forms of life that thrive and expand into other territories by assimilating the various forms of negativity they encounter are those that have been institutionalised by a governmental regime. If Christianity, for example, had not been institutionalised as the form of life of the Roman Empire, first and then of various European States, it would not have gone beyond being one religious community among others, which would perhaps have dissolved as an actual community over time. This may also invite reflection on those forms of life that are nowadays considered to be characteristic of modernity, such as capitalism, which, on these assumptions, consisted of the institutionalisation of the form of life of economic maximisation by the various governments, creating the mercantilist State of the Renaissance but also the liberal capitalist initiatives of the British landlords and squires. This does not preclude that the mercantilist form of life (or State capitalism) already existed in its ontological principle (not in its concrete historical realisation) in the past, and the liberal capitalist form of life constituted potential and actual communities prior to the agricultural revolution of the sixteenth century or the industrial revolution of the eighteenth century. The latter could have been through the proto-capitalist *encomenda* during ancient Rome, 'these were in part [business activities] directed towards the acquisition of profit, and were dependent for their success directly on market opportunities. But they were not continuous enterprises operating along the lines of modern trading companies which orient their activities to a world-wide commodity market';[24] or the mercantilism of so-called political capitalism according to Weber, for whom 'ancient capitalism was based on politics, on the exploitation for private profit of the political conquests of the imperialist city-state'.[25] Both exhibit the principle of capitalism as individual maximisation of economic profits, but in both cases, their historical realisation is different between them and with regard to the historical capitalism of the modern era: on the one hand, the *encomenda*'s realisation is fundamentally limited by the lack of a global network of markets; on the other, State-based, individual mercantilism functions through the control of trade routes and goods, and thus in a monopolised rather than a free market.

---

[24] John R. Love, *Antiquity and Capitalism* (London and New York: Routledge, 2005), pp. 164-65.
[25] Max Weber, *The Agrarian Sociology of Ancient Civilizations* (London, New Left Books, 1976), p. 364. In another place he said: 'The politically and monopolistically oriented capitalism, and even the early mercantilistic capitalism, thus came to have an interest in the creation and maintenance of the patriarchal princely power as against the estates and against the bourgeois craftsmen'. In Max Weber, *Economy and Society*, 2 vols (New York, Bedminster, 1968), II, pp. 847–48.

The second consequence, complementary to the previous one in many respects, is that non-national forms of life, those that individuals had before one of them was imposed as the national form of life, and therefore, the only one possible in the national (or supranational) territory, are under pressure to establish a relation of resistance with respect to the one imposed as exclusive, if they want to persist in their being, or, on the contrary, they are assimilated by it. How is it possible for there to be a national form of life that excludes others, and what is its ontological process of imposition? It may not seem obvious to everyone that there is a form of life that is hegemonic within a society, and, therefore, that this hegemonic form is the one institutionalised by the government. However, an intuition of this seems to be held by those who, at various times in the last century, but with particular emphasis today in the West, claim that their governments are installing communism in their country and society. And, of course, there are States whose governments have traditionally imposed a religious form of life, such as Hinduism in India and Islam in Pakistan, Saudi Arabia, etc. It would be more complex to discern, in the space we have given ourselves for this conclusion, to what extent these forms of life have already been assimilated by others, such as State or liberal capitalism, and whether, contrary to what happens with subjects, as has already been discussed, in nations there can be more than one hegemonic form of life simultaneously, or whether in fact there is no hegemonic one but only a plurality of equally valued ones. I believe that the arguments brought up against Amartya Sen's defence of the plurality of subject identities can also apply to the presumed plurality of identities of the State and the nation, which is different from attributing a plurality of identities to the society that a State encompasses, controls and limits. A nation, by definition, already since Hegel, is identified with the spirit of the people (or *Volkgeist*), i.e., the people or community has, in my terms, a particular way of being and acting. And that is the one that the government imposes on all individuals who are included within the boundaries of the State-controlled society, also on those who do not identify with it. The latter are communities that live in greater or lesser resistance to the form of life imposed on them. The nation, on the other hand, accepts the demands made on them and responds by acting accordingly with greater or lesser identification. Society is certainly plural, at least in modern States (but also in ancient States such as the great empires), but if the nation, which is the community that stands for the State, were plural, it could not survive. Take, for example, the case of the French State, a State that is currently non-denominational and secular, in which, in the first instance, it could be taken as a plural State, in which there is no dominant or hegemonic form of life, but in which the various communities coexist harmoniously making their own life, be it the Muslim religious, the Jewish religious, the Christian religious, the artistic, the philosophical, the decadent, the austere, the capitalist, etc. And yet, the demand and the commitment to defend one's own form of life (in the common expression and meaning of 'way of life') appears on numerous occasions in the speeches of French and European political leaders in general. Remember that the Head of the European Commission, Ursula von der Leyen, has recently titled the European Union Head Official for overseeing migration into the continent the 'Vice-Presidency for the Protection of our European Way of life',[26] and the French EU Presidency, in 'its EU memo warned of the dangers of "an insider culture" in some communities in Europe "that leads to rejection of the European way of life and values".'[27] But if France is a plural State in which all forms of life can have their place, what is the form of life that they claim to defend as proper to the French State or, by extension, to the European supra-State (EU)?[28] I will not venture now to propose an answer that would require much more space for its development. But, whatever this form of life that European political leaders mention, it is one and not a plurality; it is one with values, freedoms and responsibilities discernible from those of other forms of life which, nevertheless, may also be present in European society, only in a marginal way with respect to the nation and always as forms totally or partially assimilated to the national one. This assimilation strategy (and policy) can be perceived in the 2009 French State bill to ban the Muslim veil in public,[29] building on the 2004 ban of showing conspicuous religious signs, which served as a legal precedent for the local ban of the 'burkini' on the French Riviera in 2016.[30]

If, as has been said, institutionalisation is the process by which a governmental regime converts a form of life into a national one, that is, a particular way of being and acting which, in turn, expresses the image of being human with which a community of subjects identifies itself, then we must ask whether this process is the same in all cases or whether, on the contrary, it has several types. The process of institutionalising a form of life consists fundamentally of officially imposing the actions arising from an anthropical image as the necessary behaviour with which the nation expresses its way of being, its spirit. This imposition of habits, as Norbert Elias studied, goes from the elites to the

---

[26] European Commission, 'Promoting our Way of Life', https://commission.europa.eu /strategy-and-policy/priorities-2019-2024/promoting-our-european-way-life_en [accessed 29 October 2023].

[27] Andrew Rettman, 'France Pushes "European Way of Life" Amid Macron Re-election Bid', *Euobserver*, 8 February 2022 https://euobserver.com/rule-of-law/154306 [accessed 29 October 2023].

[28] Theodore Dalrymple, 'The European Way of Life', *Law and Liberty*, 24 September 2019 https:// lawliberty.org/the-european-way-of-life/ [accessed 30 October 2023].

[29] Alia Al-Saji, 'The racialization of Muslim Veils: A Philosophical Analysis', in *Philosophy and Social Criticism*, 36:8 (2010). https://doi.org/10.1177/0191453710375589.

[30] Helen Ngo, *Habits of Racism: A Phenomenology of Racism and Racialized Embodiment* (London and New York: Lexington Book, 2017), p. 28.

followers, whether they are subjects or non-subjects. And the follower-imitators spread it among themselves by imposing on each other what they are in a way predisposed to accept but also on those others who resist. Texts and other discourses, such as laws, promote certain practices and condemn others; for example, as mentioned above, in France a decree law banned the wearing or displaying of religious symbols in public, emphasising the non-religiousness of the French nation (even if there are individuals who are), and in 2021 the Chinese State banned private tutoring —especially that of English language—,[31] barred foreign curricula and ownership in some private schools[32] and it is considering the elimination of English as a compulsory subject in primary school,[33] thus emphasising the nationalistic and, as we have said, benefit-maximising character of the State as an individual entity (or Fascism),[34] while opposing the cosmopolitan and liberal character that the use of English implies. With measures such as these, the habits and attitudes of society are being brought into line with those of the nation.

But how many types of institutionalisation can there be? In recent and not-so-recent history, at least three types of State institutionalisation of the form of life can be inferred, depending on whether the society is homogeneous or heterogeneous, and on the type of heterogeneity involved. If the society is very homogeneous, so that it is made up of a single community, in the transition from tribe and chiefdom to State with the creation of a bureaucratic government,[35] the latter institutionalises the form of life of the community and

---

[31] CGTN, 'China Bans Tutoring Institutions in Core Schools Subjects From IPO', 24 July 2021, https://news.cgtn.com/news/2021-07-24/China-issues-document-to-regulate-aft er-school-tutoring-12a4svQVeH6/ index.html [accessed 30 October 2023].

[32] Muralikumar Anantharaman, 'China Bars Foreign Curricula, Ownership in Some Private Schools', *Reuters*, 17 May 2021, https://www.reuters.com/world/china/china-bars-foreign-curriculum-ownership-some-private-schools-2021-05-17/, [accessed 30 October 2023].

[33] Liu Caiyu, 'Chinese Lawmaker Proposes Removing English as Core Subject', *Global Times*, 5 March 2021, https://www.globaltimes.cn/page/202103/1217396.shtml, [accessed 29 October 2023]; and Zou Shuo, 'Debate Rages Over Proposal to Ax English', *China Daily*, 8 March 2021 https://www.chinadaily.com.cn/a/202103/08/WS6045 7153a31024ad0baad7 56.html [accessed 29 October 2023].

[34] For a discussion on fascist ideology see my *Forms of Life: Propaganda and Ideology* (Cambridge: Ethics Press, 2023).

[35] See Levellen, *Political anthropology: An Introduction*, Foreword by Victor Turner (Westport, Connecticut: Praeger, 2003): 'Many of the groups traditionally studied by anthropologists possess little that could be called government, at least not in the sense of a permanent political elite. In most nonstate systems, power is fragmentary and temporary, dispersed among families, bands, lineages, and various associations (...) Although politics is constant in such societies as individuals seek support for leadership positions, public decisions are made, and territory is defended, it is not manifested in either a monopoly of

this as a nation. This is the pure ideal case. In this case, society, nation and community coincide. The imposition is self-imposed in the whole process by

---

coercive force nor in any form of centralized economic system based on taxes or tribute'. (p. 22). For a criticism of the linear and progressive historical transformation from band to State, see David Graeber and David Wengrow, *The Dawn of Everything. A New History of Humanity* (London, UK: Allen Lane, Penguin Books Limited, 2021). They based on the alternative political and economic system of the Nambikwara of Brazil: 'It's easy to see why the neo-evolutionists of the 1950s and 1960s might not have known quite what to do with this legacy of fieldwork observations. They were arguing for the existence of discrete stages of political organization – successively: bands, tribes, chiefdoms, States – and held that the stages of political development mapped, at least very roughly, on to similar stages of economic development: hunter-gatherers, gardeners, farmers, industrial civilization. It was confusing enough that people like the Nambikwara seemed to jump back and forth, over the course of the year, between economic categories. The Cheyenne, Crow, Assiniboine or Lakota would appear to jump regularly from one end of the political spectrum to the other. They were a kind of band/State amalgam. In other words, they threw everything askew.' (pp. 119-20). And 'you can't speak of an evolution from band to tribe to chiefdom to State if your starting points are groups that move fluidly between them as a matter of habit' (pp. 121-22). I believe that, following the structure proposed by the ontology of forms of life, this combination of systems indicates that it is not the economic or the political (in the sense of social organisation) that is foundational, but the image of the human being and the ontological principle that is the law of that image: in given material conditions with strident changes of climate, vegetation and food, while a collectivist form of profit maximisation would accumulate food and resources for the season of drought and famine, and a collectivist form of survival would live in the present by using the resources of both seasons, persisting in living on the edge, a form of life harmonious with nature would realise its image of being human like the Nambikwuara, adapting both its social organisation and its economy to the dispositions of the natural seasons in a versatile way. In any case, if, as Graeber and Wengrow tell us, following Levi-Strauss, communities in the same area but different from the Nambikwara have a different way of acting, it may not simply be due to material conditions but to something else, something else that could be their image of being human, their consciousness of what is the best form of life possible in these material conditions, which in turn reveal possibilities not evident to any community, i.e. these material conditions, as Fichte would say, are constituted together with the consciousness of their form of life. As for the Eskimos, unity in these non-State communities is based on their form of life, that is, through the principle that drives and guides their customs and habits; with them 'as with the !Kung [Bushmen], maintenance of order derived from the power of custom and public opinion' (in Levellen, *Political Anthropology*, p. 26). Where these aspects are also cohesive for State communities, in the latter the government's right to coersion and to use of violence are maily instruments to reinforce that unity and especially against those individuals, communities and elements not yet assimilated. Levellen wrote: 'Because of the vast range of individual and class interests within a State, pressures and conflicts unknown in less complex societies necessitate some sort of rule of impersonal law, backed by physical sanctions, for the ongoing maintenance of the system', in *Political Anthropology*, p. 36.

each of the subjects. It would be difficult to find a pure historical case, for by definition, the State comes into being in complex societies where there is stratification and heterogeneity.[36] The closest that we can think of it may be those monarchies called 'early States' by Claessen and Skalník, such as the Yoruba of Nigeria (1400-1900 AD),[37] the Inca of Peru (1425-1532 AD)[38] or the Angkor of Cambodia (1150-1300 AD)[39] in which the king maintains the habits and rites (i.e., the ideology) proper to his community-nation through 'a centralized socio-political organization for the regulation of social relations in a complex, stratified society divided into at least two basic strata, or emergent social classes —viz. *the rulers and the ruled*—whose relations are characterized by political dominance of the former and tributary obligations of the latter, *legitimized by a common ideology*'.[40] In this case, there would not be discordant foreign elements, but rather, it would be the culmination of an autonomous social development, implying a complete assimilation of other tribes or chiefdoms. However, according to anthropologists, the most frequent type is that in which a foreigner is instituted as king or leader of the community, [41] mostly through marriage ties.[42] In this way, the foreign king or leader imposes or tries to impose his own form of life and that of his cohort of followers on the host community, transforming it by assimilation or clearly creating a complex society in which various forms of life face each other: the old and conservative

---

[36] Levellen, *Political Anthropology*, p. 48.

[37] Richard P. Schaedel, 'Early State of the Incas', in *The Early State*, ed. by Claessen and Skalník (The Hague, The Netherlands: Mouton, 1978), pp. 289-320.

[38] Natalia B. Koshakoba, 'Yoruba City-State', in *The Early State*, ed. by Claessen and Skalník (The Hague, The Netherlands: Mouton, 1978), pp. 495-510.

[39] Leonid A. Sedov, 'Angkor: Society and State', in *The Early State*, ed. by Claessen and Skalník (The Hague, The Netherlands: Mouton, 1978), pp. 111-130.

[40] Henri Claessen and Peter Skalník, 'The Early State: Models and Reality', in *The Early State*, ed. by Claessen and Skalník (The Hague, The Netherlands: Mouton, 1978), pp. 637-656 (p. 640). Italics are mine. However, according to these authors, stratification between rulers and ruled per se is not a feature of the State, since it appears also in non-State organisations, which confirms the community structure I have been arguing for (see *The Early State*, pp. 33, 350). In fact, none of the features mentioned in the quotation are in themselves signs of the primitive State, but only when all or most of them appear together.

[41] David Graeber and Marshall Sahlins, *On Kings* (Chicago: Hau Books, 2017), p. 5. 'Stranger-kingdoms are the dominant form of premodern State the world around, perhaps the original form. The kings who rule them are foreign by ancestry and identity'.

[42] David Graeber and Marshall Sahlins, *On Kings*, p. 6. 'Sovereignty is embodied and transmitted in the native woman, who constitutes the bond between the foreign intruders and the local people.'

form of the ancestors is opposed to the new foreign form then imposed as 'civilising'. This is the second type of institutionalization:

> The polity is in any case dual: divided between rulers who are foreign by nature —perpetually so, as a necessary condition of their authority— and the underlying autochthonous people, who are the 'owners' of the country. The dual constitution is constantly reproduced in narrative and ritual, even as it is continuously enacted in the *differential functions, talents, and powers of the ruling aristocracy and the native people*. (...) The superiority of the ruling aristocracy was not engendered by the process of state formation so much as *the State was engendered by the a priori superiority of an aristocracy from elsewhere*—endowed by nature with a certain *libido dominandi. The ruling class precedes and makes a subject class*.[43]

This second type of institutionalisation would occur thus in a heterogeneous society, with 'differential functions, talents, and powers'. Apart from the ancient monarchies, in the modern world, there are two options for this type of institutionalization: the first is that a minority community, such as the Nazi party followers in Germany in 1932, imposes itself on the other communities, including the Jewish community, through the government. In this example, it is a democratic government institutionalising a fascist form of life that I have called maximisation of the overall benefits of the State as an individual entity or sacrifice of the individual for the State. The second option of this second type would be that of a majority community which, through the government, claims its position in society, thus imposing its form of life from the State elites on those minority forms of life which enter into a relationship of resistance-assimilation with it. The latter case could be exemplified by the ascension to parliament in 1832 of the bourgeoisie or the so-called middle class in England, which begins to influence the making of laws in favour of the form of life that we could call, as I have argued elsewhere, the institutionalisation of the form of life of maximising individual economic profits, characteristic of incipient capitalism in the industrial era. The bourgeoisie or middle class imposed this form of life from the government as an expanding community (this is Gramsci's idea of imposing *hegemony* from a government position, thus a top-down strategy), so that by the end of the nineteenth century, a large part of the population could be considered middle class and therefore behaved as such. In this sense, the difference is that the form of life that is institutionalised by the government is not that of a minority, as in the case of Nazism, but that of a growing community

---

[43] David Graeber and Marshall Sahlins, *On Kings*, p. 5. Italics are mine.

that by its moment of splendour, dominates socially and manages to control the government (until then, at the end of the nineteenth century, under the power of the aristocracy). This can be compared to regime change through the support of the majority community whose form of life was made impossible by the imposition of government, as anthropologists tell us: 'Even in the case of major kingdoms, such as Benin or the Mexica, the initiative may indeed come from the indigenous people, who solicit a prince from a powerful outside realm. Some of what passes for "conquest" in tradition or the scholarly literature consists of usurpation of the previous regime rather than violence against the native population'.[44]

After these three general types of institutionalisation of a form of life, we come to a point that has been of great controversy in political and State theories throughout the history of thought. I refer to the issue of the legitimacy of the State. Once again, I insist that I only want to draw the fundamental consequences of the theoretical lines set out in the book with respect to the form of life as power and its relation to the State. Therefore, I do not commit myself to a systematic exposition in these following lines, but only wish to point out that, if what has been said so far is accepted, only in the case where society, nation and State coincide, can one speak of an absolute set of subjects who identify themselves with the national form of life. Otherwise, i.e., in heterogeneous societies, the State is always built on a nation that does not cover all members of society, so that the State imposes itself on them as a constraint and an obligation rather than a desired possibility. This makes the community resist a subjectivity and an identity with which they do not identify. The nation is thus reduced to a number of subjects for whom the State establishes itself as protector and vindicator of their way of being and acting, which they consider to be the best possible, while the communities of the subjects who do not constitute the nation seek to resist the process of their assimilation.

If a legitimate State is defined as one whose will-to-be is rooted in that of its members, and having asserted that the State is that of a society which it controls and delimits, one would have to qualify as illegitimate any State in which there is no coincidence between nation and society. A State whose society is heterogeneous would not be legitimate, because its non-national communities do not have the same will-to-be as the nation that has been institutionalised by the government. This would be a return to the classical theory

---

[44] David Graeber and Marshall Sahlins, *On Kings*, p. 6.

of anarchism, [45] as long as one takes into account that there are postulate cases, however ideal they may seem to us, in which nation and society coincide and therefore in which living under a State would be legitimate. Legitimacy is here derived from the will-to-be of individuals and not from the institutional procedure of government, in opposition to the processualist theories of the modern age. The State is not legitimate because it has emerged from a neutral legal procedure but because it responds to the will of each of those who can call themselves subjects of the national form of life institutionalised by the government. In this sense, from the ontology of the forms of life it is possible to connect with the Rousseaunian theories of the general will[46] in a more comprehensive study of the matter.

A very particular case that many European citizens, especially in Western Europe, have experienced in this regard is the assimilation of the *Roma or Gypsy community*[47] into the liberal capitalist form of life. The subjects of this community struggled for centuries to live according to their image of being human; they were wandering people [48] always in conflict with the authorities of the places where they arrived, and where they were frequently subjected to

---

[45] For a discussion on the idea of Anarchism, see Noam Chomsky, 'Notes on Anarchism', in *Chomsky on Anarchism,* selected and edited by Barry Pateman (Edinburgh, Oakland, West Virginia: AK Press, 2005), pp. 118-32. And in the same volume, 'Containing the Threat of Democracy' (pp. 153-77), Chomsky refers to Russell on Anarchism: 'Those who adopt the common sense principle that freedom is our natural right and essential need will agree with Bertrand Russell that anarchism is "the ultimate ideal to which society should approximate". Structures of hierarchy and domination are fundamentally illegitimate. They can be defended only on grounds of contingent need, an argument that rarely stands up to analysis'. (p. 156).

[46] Taylor, *Modern Social Imaginaries*: 'True harmony can come only when we overcome this duality, when my love of myself coincides with my desire to fulfil the legitimate goals of my co-agents (those participating with me in this harmonization). In Rousseau's language, the primitive instincts of self-love (*amour de soi*) and sympathy (*pitié*) fuse together in the rational and virtuous human being into a love of the common good, which in the political context is known as the general will' (p. 117).

[47] I will use both terms interchangeably.

[48] It has been debated for centuries whether the Gypsies are in fact a single ethnic group or a rable of various communities/nations. Today there seems to be a consensus that they are a people originating in northern India, as their language seems to be derived from Hindi. However, the reason for their departure from India, or even the reason for their wandering over the centuries since at least the twelfth century, is not understood. In line with what is shown in the following paragraphs, it could be said that wandering is not essential to these people, but that it is precisely their fervent resistance to assimilation that has made them always live on the margins and move from place to place frequently.

expulsion orders, imprisoned or killed.[49] In the last century, they continue to live as in the past in large families with marked endogamy; they were more or less marginalised in the labour sphere, or they got so-called small jobs that did not compromise their identity and their wandering status (as travellers). Their children did not go to school, and still, in the twenty-first century, this is a problem to be solved.[50] Large families lived in dubious hygienic conditions[51] in small houses, in tends or in caravans on the outskirts of an urban area or in suburbs (as the unauthorized nomad camps outside Rome, Milan and Naples),[52] practically continuously exposed to the public street where, by personal experience, it was not unusual to see some of them selecting objects in rubbish bins or scavenging through rubble in search of something to sell in a street market. In short, it was not a capitalist life, but rather, due to the important role of the family and its inherent patriarchy, I would dare to describe it as a maximisation of the general goods and benefits of the family as an individual entity —bearing in mind that because of the acute endogamy their families tend to be the merger of several families, which makes them be close to a clan.

The Gypsy community today has different degrees of assimilation into the liberal capitalist form of life depending on the country they live in. In general,

---

[49] Kalwant Bhopal and Martin Myers, *Insiders, Outsiders and Others. Gypsies and Identity* (Hatfield, Hertfordshire: University of Hertfordshire Press, 2008), pp. 179-80. See also, Shulamith Shahar, 'Religious Minorities, Vagabonds and Gypsies in Early Modern Europe', in *The Roma. A Minority in Europe. Historical, Political and Social Perspectives*, ed. by Roni Stauber and Raphael Vago (Budapest and New York: Central European University Press, 2007), pp. 1-18.

[50] Andrew Richard Ryder, Iulius Rostas & Marius Taba, '"Nothing about us without us": the role of inclusive community development in school desegregation for Roma communities', *Race Ethnicity and Education*, 17:4 (2014), pp. 518-39, http://dx.doi.org/10.1080/13613324.2014.885426.

[51] Vanessa Heaslip, Denise Wilson and Debra Jackson, 'Are Gypsy Roma Traveller communities indigenous and would identification as such better address their public health needs?' *Public Health* 176 (2019), 43-49 https://doi.org/10.1016/.puhe.2019.0 2.020

[52] At these 'nomad camps', attacks by various groups (neo-Nazis, camorra gangs and angry residents) occurred following allegations that a young Roma woman had attempted to kidnap a baby. This highlights the perennial association of the Roma community with crime and social disruption. These mentioned episodes let to the 'Maroni Census': 'This census would, according to the government, make the people living in these nomad camps "visible" by creating a database with their fingerprints and other information that would allow for their identification.' See Susana Martínez Guillem, 'European Identity: Across Which Lines? Defining Europe Through Public Discourses on the Roma', *Journal of International and Intercultural Communication*, 4:1 (2011), 23-41 (p. 24).

in Western Europe, and especially in Spain, Portugal and Germany,[53] they have been assimilated through marrying non-Roma individuals and holding salaried jobs with a view to consumption and the use of modern technologies. This assimilation was a triumph of capitalism and, in a way, the beginning of the end of the Roma community in Western Europe. This has created a certain distinction between those assimilated Gypsies, who are considered citizens with whom the subjects of the majority community believe they share the same form of life, and those other Gypsies who have not assimilated, and who continue to be defamed, rejected and denounced in public speeches such as the one in the British newspaper *The Sun*, where it is said that 'they do not have a 'quarrel' with the 'settled Gipsy' population', [54] suggesting that the latter 'are Gypsies who once would have been defined by their difference but are now subsumed within the values and lifestyles of Sun readers',[55] while non-assimilated Gypsies seem to be anathema, because as absolute-Others with their negative form of life, 'they are shaped as living their lives irrevocably outside the values of Sun readers [all-embracing Middle Englanders]; the impossibility of living next door to such characters is absolute, their presence is an infringement into the lives of dominant society and they need to be cast out'.[56] In the digital age, this discriminatory discourse against the Roma community has taken the form of hate speech on social networks such as Twitter, which has sparked a debate about how far freedom of expression goes and to what extent it is an instrument of assimilation of the Other by the hegemonic community.[57]

On the other hand, the assimilation of the Roma community,[58] and thus their dissolution in the majority community, has led to an increase in the favourable

---

[53] Botond Csepregi, 'Gypsies in Europe', interview to Szilveszter Póczik (published originally in Hungarian in *Confessio*, 4 (2010). Translated by *Reformed Church in Hungary*, https://reformatus.hu/english/news/gypsies-in-europe_poczik/ [accessed 29 October 2023].

[54] Kalwant Bhopal and Martin Myers, *Insiders, Outsiders and Others. Gypsies and Identity* (Hatfield, Hertfordshire: University of Hertfordshire Press, 2008), p. 185.

[55] Kalwant Bhopal and Martin Myers, *Insiders, Outsiders and Others*, p. 185.

[56] Kalwant Bhopal and Martin Myers, *Insiders, Outsiders and Others*, p. 185.

[57] Therese Enarssona and Simon Lindgrenb, 'Free speech or hate speech? A legal analysis of the discourse about Roma on Twitter', *Information and Communications Technology Law*, 28 (2018) https://doi.org/10.1080/ 13600834.2018.1494415.

[58] 'On many occasions, however, they were settled somewhere, and as a consequence, they gradually lost their Gypsy characteristics, the outsider's attitude and became assimilated.' In Botond Csepregi, 'Gypsies in Europe', *Reformed Church in Hungary*, https://reformatus.hu/english/news/gypsies-in-europe_poczik/ [accessed 29 October 2023]. It is an interview to Szilveszter Póczik, published originally in Hungarian in *Confessio*, 4 (2010).

opinion of other citizens in these countries.[59] However, the problem remains, because, according to some historians, the Roma have not only lived and continue to live on the margins of society, but generally following its laws and principles of purity,[60] resist their assimilation into the form of life of the host national community[61] and shun State coercion.[62] According to this and following my arguments above, it can be said that for the non-assimilated Roma community, the State is illegitimate, and so is the force it uses to keep them under the discipline of the desirable and necessary habits of the nation (schooling, regular paid work, private property in registered domicile, payment of taxes, freedom of choice of marriage for women, etc.). The latter brings us back to the argument of the liberal State and its claim to neutrality and even multiculturalism, for, as the case of the Gypsies shows, different cultures can only coexist as long as in the public space of everyday life, they all act according to the 'normal' way, i.e., the hegemonic form of life. But 'if one group's culture is identified to behave in a different way, one that falls outside such parameters, then such behaviour needs to be treated differently'[63], for the *difference blindness* of the liberal and multicultural State '(it) assumes that the minority culture will exhibit the same behaviour patterns or acquiesce to those behaviour patterns that are preferred by the dominant society [I would say dominant community]'.[64]

Finally, I think it is interesting to ask, albeit experimentally with a view to a more extensive analysis in a later work, what are the possible combinations that

---

[59] Pew Research Center, 'EU View of Roma, Muslim, Jews', In *A Fragile Rebound for EU Image on Eve of European Parliament Elections.* Report 12 May 2014 https://www.pew research.org /global/2014/05/12/chapter-4-views-of-roma-muslims-jews/, [accessed 29 October 2023]: 'In Germany, since 1991, unfavorable sentiment toward Roma has declined from 60% to 42%. In Spain, over the same period, it has fallen from 50% to 41%.'

[60] Shulamith Shahar, 'Religious Minorities, Vagabonds and Gypsies in Early Modern Europe', in *The Roma. A Minority in Europe. Historical, Political and Social Perspectives*, ed. by Roni Stauber and Raphael Vago (Budapest and New York: Central European University Press, 2007), pp. 1-18. 'It is also difficult to assess the frequency of mixed marriages, given that the Gypsies on the whole tended to keep apart from the gadjo (external, non-Gypsy) world, and that their purity laws greatly restricted their contacts with non-Gypsies' (p. 10)

[61] 'Gypsies, however, did not want condescension. It would be a mistake to think that they were incapable of adaptation. It is more likely that they lacked the will to integrate, so they insisted on a peripheric and liberal form of existence'. In Botond Csepregi, 'Gypsies in Europe', *Reformed Church in Hungary*, https://reformatus.hu/english/ne ws/gypsies-in-europe_poczik/ [accessed 29 October 2023].

[62] Shulamith Shahar, 'Religious Minorities, Vagabonds and Gypsies in Early Modern Europe', p. 12.

[63] Kalwant Bhopal and Martin Myers, *Insiders, Outsiders and Others*, p. 181.

[64] Kalwant Bhopal and Martin Myers, *Insiders, Outsiders and Others*, p. 181.

can constitute a State, and whether the type of regime conditions the form of life imposed and vice versa. This last question, from our ontological perspective, can shed light on what can be expected about a governmental regime. For example, it is possible in this light to analyse the false expectation that the US had regarding China's democratisation when they intensified their relations at the end of the twentieth century, and the intensification of that expectation following the former's invitation to the latter to join the World Trade Organisation (WTO) and thus its entry into the global free market.

It is interesting to recognise the relevance of the question of the relationship between regime and form of life, if only briefly, because, as Fukuyama famously predicted, the perfect and indissoluble union of democracy and capitalism as the 'end of history'.[65] It seemed then that there were indeed governments, such as the democratic one, that were better qualified, if you like, to establish and promote certain forms of life, such as the capitalist one. This was called into question by China's unstoppable advance into the capitalist market economy following its aforementioned entry into the WTO.[66] What conclusions could be drawn, even tentatively, from the ontology of forms of life? In principle, as the recent Chinese case attests, there does not seem to be a relationship of necessity between forms of life and governmental regimes. Any kind of form of life can be institutionalised by any kind of government, so it does not seem that there are governments that are intrinsically better suited to some forms of life than others and that, in any case, what makes them more or less successful is the social and material condition in which their combination is realised.[67] History shows us monarchies that institutionalised religious forms of life, such as the medieval theocracy; monarchies that institutionalised humanistic forms of life that pursued the maximisation of individual goods and pleasures, such as some Renaissance monarchies and city-States; monarchies that institutionalised forms of life in harmony with nature such as that of the Inca,

---

[65] Francis Fukuyama, *The End of History and the Last Man* (New York: The Free Press, 1992), pp. 109-25. 'Looking around the world, there remains a very strong overall correlation between advancing socio-economic modernization and the emergence of new democracies. Traditionally the most economically advanced regions, Western Europe and North America, have also hosted the world's oldest and most stable liberal democracies'. (p. 112)

[66] Kerry Brown, *China's World. What Does China Want?* (London and New York: I. B. Tauris, 2017), pp. 33-34.

[67] China's success was not, as is widely believed, only due to the combination of capitalism with government centralisation, for this combination in itself would not have succeeded without a free market that Chinese companies heavily subsidised by the government took advantage of.

Aztec and Mayan kings, and even the project of a monarchy that institutionalised the philosophical form of life such as Plato's ideal city.

The same can be said of the various types of democratic governments and the different forms of life they have institutionalised, such as the democracy of the Athenian republic, which promoted a humanistic life of individual development through the exploitation of all spheres of human life, all its goods and pleasures. Or the American democracy of individual maximisation of economic profits. Or the incipient phase of French democracy of liberation and libertarianism, chaos and disorder, destruction and euphoria, which can hardly be understood except as a form of life of alienation, a constant unattainable desire to cancel one's self-consciousness, a flight from oneself. So in the euphoria of its beginnings, and until the terror of Robespierre and Marat, the people, the nation institutionalized by that French revolutionary government, sought to forget what it was, its deep certainty that it was a great void, pure possibility of possibilities, and then pretended to be something necessarily and legitimately, pretended above all that all men (of its nation and community called in populist discourse 'the people')[68] were sovereign subjects like kings and lords and they competed for their share, as Taylor says on the division of society during the first years of the French Revolution, 'what made these latter divisions so deadly was the absence of any agreed understanding on the institutional meaning of the sovereignty of the nation'.[69]

The examples of different historical combinations of regimes and forms of life are innumerable. But there is no objection in principle to non-historical combinations being perfectly viable, such as, for example, a philosophical democracy or an oligarchy of artists. That they are feasible here does not bind me to the effectiveness of their historical realisation as a State. Plato's failures in the realisation of his State model in Syracuse are well known. Obviously, as in the examples given, each combination ultimately depends on the material conditions in which it is realised, so that its realisation will vary, though not essentially, according to these conditions and of the power of the form of life to create its own conditions. Among these conditions can be taken the number of inhabitants in a society. A capitalist democracy in societies that are not overpopulated could equally well be a capitalist democracy in a society with a very large population. The end result varies, but the essential principle remains. Contemporary India is a case in point. This is at odds with the negative diagnosis that the CCP's discourse apparatus has attributed to an elective, parliamentary democracy in mainland China precisely because of the huge

---

[68] Laclau, Ernesto, *On Populist Reason* (London and New York: Verso, 2005).
[69] Taylor, *Modern Social Imaginaries*, p. 113.

population of its society, a diagnosis that indirectly wants to justify the present type of authoritarian oligarchic regime.[70]

A more sophisticated approach is that of the Chinese philosopher Jiwei Ci, for whom the establishment of a democratic government in China would face 4 challenges:[71] 1. democracy must be born out of the internal reform of the CCP itself, as it is the only party allowed in China and the alternative to this reform is a non-peaceful revolution. 2. As Chinese citizens and society have been kept under 'compulsory moral tutelage by the party', they have been prevented from acquiring any 'independent moral agency', one that is 'attributable to their own initiative' and over which the communist party has no 'prerogative of guidance and control', once the population is freed from such 'guidance and control', a moral crisis is expected in the sense of behaviour not driven by fear of punishment but also not by any moral principles. 3. Given its willingness to stage political change towards democracy, weakening its 'centripetal capacity' would unleash 'unprecedented opportunities for all separatist tendencies to expand' and become more aggressive towards their goal. 4. The last challenge, according to Ci, has to do with the combination of democracy and capitalism, for if, on the one hand, political democratisation would lead citizens to want to participate in government, on the other hand, capitalism, understood in the liberal sense, would exacerbate social inequality and cause the capitalist class to 'capture the State for their corporate interest' away from ordinary citizens expectations. Notwithstanding these challenges, the author presents democracy as necessary to legitimise the Chinese communist party, for this is the ultimate goal, the Machiavellian 'mantenere lo stato'. But the State requires a form of life in addition to government; hence, democracy is needed to legitimise it. For, according to Ci, Chinese society is already largely democratic; he says that citizens are allowed to express themselves and contribute to society with their acquired skills, and that everyone can decide for themselves what good life they want to pursue 'subject only to reasonable and reasonably permissive laws'.[72] It should be noted that the latter is in direct contradiction with his own assertion that without 'party guidance and control', Chinese society would be in crisis, as *its citizens have not developed any kind of moral agency of their own.*

---

[70] Alice Yan, 'Hongkongers living in mainland China say safety and friendships are on the line amid protests', *South Cina Morning Post*, 16 December 2019 https://www.scmp.com/news/china/society/article/3041417/hongkongers-living-mainland-china-say-safety-and-friendships-are?module=perpetual_scroll_0&pgtype=article&campaign = 3041417 [accessed 29 October 2023].

[71] Jiwei Ci, *Democracy in China. The Coming Crisis* (London and Massachusetts: Havard University Press, 2019), pp. 22-29.

[72] Ci, *Democracy in China*, p. 21.

Thus, Ci's argument is that a society undergoing an 'inevitable process of democratisation' can only fit a political system that is also democratic, and therefore, the government must be reformed in such a way that citizens have a greater say in it. One should note, however, that what this author seems to mean by 'democratic society' does not correspond to the reality of today's Chinese society, where neither freedom of expression nor the possibility to lead one's chosen good life (e.g., religious) due to government interference in the life of the individuals who do not put the interests of the State first and foremost. And if it is not accepted that Chinese society is already somehow democratic, it follows that the need for a democratic government cannot be accepted either. It is by discussing this suggestion that I would like to end this section, for I hope it will help me to make it clearer that the lack of legitimisation of the State is the norm in complex societies and that there is no need for a particular type of government, since it is not the result of natural or historical law but of human will and is therefore contingent, as self-imposed by a community.

Taking the case of China and its State, legitimation in Jiwei Ci's theory is justified —as a discourse— by a historical law not dissimilar to that of historical materialism, whereby a society becomes more democratic as it advances. One has to recognise in the way he defines a democratic society an emphasis on otherwise Marxist characteristics such as 'eradication of a fixed social hierarchy' or 'fixed class distinctions' and their replacement with 'equality of conditions'.[73] Thus, in order to be legitimate, the State has to respond to this inherent tendency in the modern social-historical process, which, according to the author, China would have joined thanks to the CCP. His argument, however, does not seem to be in line with that of the leaders in Beijing, who have recently pushed for greater centralisation, as well as an intensification of nationalism and an expansion of their communist base throughout Chinese society. Instead of stepping aside to decentralise the political life of the Chinese citizen, the State has intensified its control. This is because they have realised that legitimisation comes not from the political process —the CCP came to power after a bloody civil war and maintained itself through external imposition, coercion and assimilation of ever larger sections of society— but from the whole of society identifying with the guiding principle imposed by the government and integrating as a nation. And this as the result of Propaganda and imposition; with the one, it allows the self-affirmation and identification of each citizen with the government and its projects, which, in the end, seek the maximisation of the general goods of the State as an individual entity and thus of the nation identified with the State; the other makes it impossible to realise behaviour and hopes other than those envisaged by the State and the form of

---

[73] Jiwei Ci, *Democracy in China*, pp. 20-21.

life that constitutes it, so that citizens gradually identify themselves with the ends of the State, to the extent that individuals are prepared to sacrifice themselves for these ends, until blind obedience has been formed. This legitimisation does not require democracy, so to think that arguments like Jiwei Ci's can bend the will of the Chinese State elites is pure illusion, and frankly very näive. On the other hand, what is necessary is only the will with which they impose on themselves the form of life and type of government. It is not the one-party, oligarchic rule of the CCP that seems likely to change in the future, but Chinese society, which will become even more 'democratic', not in the sense of Ci, but in the sense of more egalitarian with respect to the ends of the State, for which all individuals are equally to be sacrificed for its maintenance.

The Chinese case can thus illustrate that there is no need for one type of government or another, but only a will, because its choice depends on an elite installed in the government, which will maintain the characteristics of the latter as the crystallisation of a fixed and immovable will. One can, with this example, discern the two constituents of the State, its form of life and its government; and it can be understood that the ultimate impossible legitimacy has its source in the community of subjects, hence the importance of propaganda, imposition (censorship, disappearance of persons, coercion, etc., which shorten the way to total assimilation)[74] and the strategy of assimilation, all of which brings with it the coveted social stability. But if you can penetrate my words, you will understand that the structure of the legitimisation of all governments, including democratic ones, is embedded in this model. Indeed, no one today can question the fact that democratic governments seem to lack legitimacy in the eyes of large portions of a country's population. In the US elections in 2020, in the German elections in 2021, in the French elections in 2022, etc., there is a division and polarisation that clearly shows that for about 50% of the population, the democratically elected government does not represent them.

Perhaps the lesson is that the West has congratulated itself on its system of government with full confidence in the 'democratic process' for a fair outcome and has forgotten the more important thing of nation-making, i.e., to bring into being a community identified and integrated with the same vital guiding

---

[74] The same logic inspired the CCP with regard to other issues such as the zero-covid policy: when zero-covid cannot be obtained in a locality, infected cases are removed to the outskirts so that it can be said that there are no more covid-infected people in that locality; the same applies to assimilation: when assimilation fails, it is resorted to disappearance or imprisonment.

principle, values and emotions;[75] perhaps such forgetfulness is not such, but the result of failing to recognise that despite its alleged neutrality, the liberal State imposes a vital (ontological) principle, albeit weakened precisely by its own lack of recognition and faith in it. Perhaps multiculturalism has created disengagement and abstention in a population that has been converted to different forms of life not represented by electoral candidates. Perhaps Western democratic States have gained their legitimacy in a transnational community of subjects that constitute their true nation. Perhaps the Western States have sidelined communities in resistance beyond this aforementioned liberal capitalist transnational community —along with subjects from non-Western countries— that holds them together so that this is the true 'nation' they have institutionalised as hegemonic. But if this is so, the West is only a small portion of what it could be. On the other hand, and paradoxical though it may seem — but it is not— in this balance of forces, between the nation and the communities that resist being it, lies the continuity and survival of the being of the Western 'nation', while in its absolute homogeneity and consolidation (after eliminating the unassimilated and impossible to assimilate) the Chinese nation will meet its doom, in which having made it impossible to doubt themselves as subjects, community and State, and thus impossible for anyone to dare to question or venture to dissent, the whole nation will leap into the abyss, as a final sacrifice (suicide or desperate movement of expansion), so that having completely won themselves, they will be lost. The difference from the West, then, is to have a robust set of communities that resist without any fundamental change in that resistance, but to persist in the never self-founded, never consolidated self, thus constituting a balance of conflicts.

With this, and drawing on what has been said, it must be concluded that if resistance brings conflict, homogenisation leads to dissolution. If it can only rarely be said that a State is legitimate, and therefore any social community that does not identify with it is right not to feel it as legitimate, legitimacy, on the other hand, like any ideal condition (universalised and totalised), is dangerous, because it entails the absence of resistance and therefore, with the negation of the Other that is one's negative constitution, one obtains the destruction of the self—as a self-negation—. This translates into those communities which, having partially overcome —in the present totality— the internal resistance of

---

[75] Eric Wolf criticizes the substantialist concept of nation and defines the process of nation making as follows: 'Instead of treating the nation as a homogeneous and ahistorical given, we should (...) on how nation buildingbrought together culturally heterogeneous populations and gradually fostered their integration into a larger structure through the proliferation of new systemwide culture patterns'. In Eric Wolf, *Pathways of Power. Building an Anthropology of the Wodern World* (London, Berkely and Los Angeles: University of California Press, 2001). p. 83.

their own negative constitution, which is that form of life from which they flee and to which they submit, end up running towards their destruction while, at the same time, in their self-foundation, they want to rescue the meaning that was lost in the negation of their constitutive opposite. The community and the subjects thus closed end up winning themselves only to lose themselves immediately afterwards. The loss is the impossibility of continuing to exist. Without the resistance presented to us by the community that exhibits our particular constitutive opposite,[76] there is no continuing to be. My aim here is only to establish the limits within which the will-to-be can continue to realise itself and outside of which it is impossible to persist in being. Within these limits is the totalising unfolding of being as the form of life of the community, nation and State. The ethics of the State is codified in the successive totalities (form of life in the present stage) fixed in this process of necessary totalisation.

State and Ethics

If the State is constituted by a governmental regime and a form of life, that is, an ideology, it is worth discussing, albeit briefly, what role ethics plays in the State: does the State have an ethical duty? The answer may be controversial, but being consistent with the foundations of this ontology, it should be affirmed that the ethical duty of the State is precisely the promotion of the form of life of the nation, understanding by ethics the behaviours considered 'normal' and 'desirable' by the national community, since living the way they live is the best possible way. As we said in the introduction, the moral imperative of the subject is the demand to perform with greater intensity and perfection the actions proper to the anthropical image with which he identifies. And this implies the demand to actualise in his actions the ontological principle that is the law of that image. Could the same not be said of the State? The duty of the State would be, according to this, to demand from citizens, subjects and non-subjects — within its society—, the realisation of a certain form of life, while the ethical discourse justifies through the media and other cultural devices their behaviours taken as necessary possibilities. For example, when it comes to those States considered capitalist, individual economic maximisation as a principle directs all those actions considered by the community as good, with the discourse of 'so much you have or so much purchasing power you have, so much you are worth'. In this sense, its ethics is related to the Calvinist and

---

[76] For an account of the constitutive opposites of each form of life, see my *Forms of life. Some Images of Human Being*. Forthcoming.

pietistic ethics studied by Weber in his well-known book,[77] an ethics that has its ontological principle in a life oriented towards economic success.

The problem with this ethics of the 'illegitimate State' is that it only responds to the ethics of the national community and not to the other communities and forms of life that are equally encompassed by the State and society. This problem obviously does not affect the legitimate State, which is a rarely attainable ideal, and which, in its own final achievement, calls for its own self-destruction —as mentioned above— for lack of the possibility of continuing to be, when even its constitutive opposites are discarded or assimilated to the hegemonic principle. Self-destruction, in this sense, has to be framed in the ultimate realisation of the principle that governs a community. Such ultimate realisation implies the progressive incarnation of the object by the subject. That is to say, the community self-destructs or predisposes itself to self-destruction as a way of realising its longed-for union with the object, which is taken as the incarnation of the anthropical image in the perfection of its temporal totality (passing into other totalities of the infinite progress of totalisation). The ethics of every form of life is thus the path towards that final sacrifice of the subject and its community as the consummation of the principle that governs them in their process of totalisation with respect to their form of life. And to put it more clearly, our ethics with respect to the good life brings us to a point where all our actions fall under that good life and its governing principle, so that once we have voluntarily submitted all our actions (overcoming indeterminacy, confusion, doubt, and the resistance of other forms of life), it only remains for us to sacrifice our actual existence in the world. Alternatively, it can be expressed as the will that the end of our existence should fully embody our ontological principle, or, if you will, that the end of our existence should serve to preserve that principle in the world for all to see. This is self-destruction.

At this point, it is necessary to emphasise the already established difference between being and existence. While the latter is sacrificed and ends, being — which is the form of life— continues to be incarnated in other subjects and other communities and times. This does not mean that one can exist without being, nor that being does not need existence for its realisation; in fact, being can only be given in existence. Without it, what remains is the principle or anthropical image as a possibility. But the subject that integrates himself in his totalisation until he is self-grounded in his present totality —identifying with it and acting as the form of life in its present state commands— tends to the ultimate sacrifice of his existence for the principle that governs him in such a way that in that moment of present sacrifice is gathered the entirety of his life's

---

[77] Max Weber, *The Protestant Ethics and the Spirit of Capitalism* (London and New York: Routledge, 2005).

time: the past in which such a principle was not obeyed is redeemed in that present, and the already impossible individual future is definitively endowed with meaning. Both the past and the future are homogenised in the present situation of positing the definitive identification between being and existence. This is the logic of the fundamentalist, who is the one who tends and finally comes to incarnate the image of the human being in its temporally fixed totality, seeking his self-foundation.[78] This erases the guilt of not having always been the subject of such a form of life and reaffirms him in his will to be, beyond even his existence.[79] Thus, the Nazi contemplates the final self-sacrifice of his

---

[78] A contemporary example may be the insistence on the use of nuclear missiles by Russian nationalists and fundamentalists in their conflict with Ukraine and the West. See 'Ukraine war: Russia's 'propaganda warriors' pushing for use of nuclear weapons, Nobel laureate warns', *South China Morning Post*, 4 May 2022 https://www.scmp.com/news/world/russia-central-asia/article/3176425/ukraine-war-russias-propaganda-warriorsar earguing?campaign=3176425&module=perpetual_scroll_0&pgtype= article [accessed 30 October 2023]. In their insistence, one can see this willingness to sacrifice their existence for the sake of the State as an individual entity, and even more so to realise in its perfection the ontological principle that governs them, for nuclear war means mutual destruction. In this ultimate sense, these fundamentalists can be put ontologically on a par with terrorists who self-immolate in order to achieve an impossible perfection in their everyday existence.

[79] It is worth distinguishing the logic of the self-sacrificer from the logic of the suicidal person. In suicide there is an attempt both to eliminate the world we have not been able to assimilate, and thus understand, and to eliminate our existence, having revealed our being/form of life as impossible to realise in this world, which is an Other in heavy resistance. Losing ourselves here does not imply gaining plural possibilities of being as in generosity, for the suicidal person voluntarily seeks to cease to exist and thus to cancel all future possibilities, indeed, the loss of his existence seeks as an ultimate goal to lose himself. Contrary to suicide, operated by the one who wants to lose his being by losing his existence, the self-sacrifice of the one who wins himself and loses his existence presupposes a longing for perfection: the homogenisation of life in its temporal succession through the ultimate realisation of the ontological principle in its present totality. In short, if suicide entails to lose the existence in order to lose oneself, the self-sacrifice entails losing the existence as the result of gaining oneself. In this sense, the self-sacrificing person is reified as the ultimate incarnation of his *anthropical image*, this not only corresponds to the example of the suicide bomber, but also to the person who, in order to win himself, mistreats or endangers his existence to the point of collapse or exhaustion, like the religious person who, in order to glorify God, carries out missions that risk his existence, or the sick writer who tirelessly seeks to express his inner world in the book he knows will be the last he writes because he puts his project before the care of his health; the one who, in order to maximise his economic profits, works to the point of exhaustion or does business that is dangerous to his existence; the one who seeks to intensify his pleasures to the extreme or the one who seeks to alienate and forget himself (his being) by means of narcotics, alcohol or other substances that end up tearing him out of his existence -this is not a suicide, however, since it is his project of forgetting his

existence for the good of the State; the artist integrated in his totalisation merges with his work of art until he disappears in it, which was brilliantly expressed by Oscar Wilde in the *Portrait of Dorian Gray*, the religious person in his ethics reaches the peak of self-immolation, ceasing to exist, for the glory of God, so that paradoxically by ceasing to exist, a more faithful realisation of his being (willingness to act for the glory of God) and greater status with respect to his community is achieved. Is this not the logic of holiness and martyrs? It can be said that the subject, by winning himself, closes in on himself, discarding at the same time his contingency and becoming a necessary being beyond his bare existence —as a cancellation of all possibility of continuing to exist— and as such loses the contingent existence of man so that an impossible god might be born.[80]

A Historical Example: Rome

The above is perhaps what happens with the Roman Empire. But why mention the Roman Empire now after having concentrated on contemporary examples? Fundamentally, it serves to show the transhistorical character of the principle and the totalising structure of the form of life. After the attempted suicide of Nero's great burning of Rome —an act also born of the quest to fix imperial Rome in its unfading image, once its real existence had been destroyed— and the conversion to Christianity after the great crisis of the third century, we have the fall of the empire in the fifth century.[81] The falling empire —maintaining

---

being that leads him to the final paroxysm and the loss of his existence, and not the opposite, the loss of existence as a means of losing himself-.

[80] Here I follow Jean-Paul Sartre when, in his *L'être et le néant*, he wrote: 'Every human reality is a passion in that it projects losing itself so as to found being and by the same stroke to constitute the In-itself which escapes contingency by being its own foundation, the Ens causa sui, which religions call God. Thus, the passion of man is the reverse of that of Christ, for man loses himself as man in order that God may be born. But the idea of God is contradictory and we lose ourselves in vain. Man is a useless passion'. In *Being and Nothingness* (New York: Philosohical Library, 1956), p. 615.

[81] It is important to note that this crisis was the prelude to the conversion of Imperial Rome to Christianity. The crisis meant a weakening of Rome's military and political (administrative) power, caused perhaps by the destabilisation and doubt brought to its form of life by Christianity and the resources invested in its persecution and rejection. Watts wrote: 'Eusebius emphasized that Christian persecutions made the empire weaker and endangered the Roman recovery that the tetrarchs claimed to be protecting'. In Edward J. Watts, *The Eternal Decline and Fall of Rome* (New York: Oxford University Press, 2021), p. 74. In addition, during the 3rd century, Christians sometimes aided the barbarians against the pagan Romans: 'In the region of Pontus in northern Asia Minor, for example, the Christian bishop Gregory 'the Wonder-Worker' (thaumatourgos in Greek) angrily rebuked members of his congregation for 'going over to the barbarians' at a time of Gothic invasion, aiding them in the murdering of their compatriots, and pointing out to the

that the empire of the West did indeed fall (something that has been questioned recently)—[82] is the Christian Roman empire. This is important because it was a 'new' empire forged with Constantine after his adherence to Christianity,[83] after uniting the different sects and factions in a common doctrine with the Council of Nicea. His wish was that Rome '(it) would be a Christian Empire and, as a second Moses, Constantine would create a new social order by leading Christians from persecution into power'.[84] A Christianity that, with Theodosius, ended up imposing itself as the religion of the empire with what this implied for the imperial bureaucracy, which essentially changed the identity of Rome. So that, if before Constantine Christians were persecuted, now, with him, those who practise the pagan religion are persecuted by means of the anti-pagan laws, temples are demolished, or they are handed over to the Church and the coffers of the latter are swollen, thus replacing the motivation of defence against enemies with progress with regard to spiritual salvation.[85] For, the defence of the borders was supported by public money, so when this practice ceased, 'both these troops and the frotier disappear'.[86] Christianity, according to Gibbon, was the original cause of the fall of Rome.[87] In connection with this

---

barbarians the 'houses most worth plundering'. A similar settling of social scores amidst military chaos and political crisis was also to be a feature of life in Rome's Western provinces'. In Peter Sarris, *Empires of Faith* (New York: Oxford University Press, 2011), p. 12. Constantine's conversion brought stability back to Rome but with a different identity. It ceased to be (what it was) and became something else, but doubt and instability did not cause it to lose its existence as an empire.

[82] Peter Heather, *The Fall of the Roman Empire. A New History of Rome and the Barbarians* (New York: Oxford University Press, 2006): 'What did come to an end in 476 was any attempt to maintain the western Roman Empire as an overarching, supra-regional political structure (...) Provincial Romanness survived in parts of the west after 476, but central Romanness was a thing of the past.' (p. 432). In The Eternal Decline and the Fall of Rome it is presented the argument that Rome did not fall in 476 A.D, 'the fall of Rome in 476 was manufactured to serve the propaganda purposes of later Romans'. It was propaganda to show Justinian as the emperor of the East destined to conquest the West and restore the Christian Roman Empire. pp. 123-24.

[83] Edward J. Watts, *The Eternal Decline and Fall of Rome* (New York: Oxford University Press, 2021), p. 74.

[84] Watts, *The Eternal Decline and Fall of Rome*, p. 75.

[85] Watts, *The Eternal Decline and Fall of Rome*, pp. 81-82.

[86] Bryan Ward-Perkins, *The Fall of Rome and the End of Civilization* (New York: Oxford University Press, 2005), pp. 18-19.

[87] Edward Gibbon, *The Decline and Fall of the Roman Empire*, ed. by J. B. Bury, 6 vols (London: Methuen & Co., 1897), IV, pp. 162-63: 'the church, and even the State, were distracted by religious factions, whose conflicts were sometimes bloody, and always implacable; the attention of emperors was diverted from camps to synods; the Roman

thesis, but without forgetting the role played by the disruptive character of the barbarian incursions in the fifth century, best exemplified by the sack of Rome in 410 A.D., it can be said that the disposition —or hope— of the Roman Christian community facilitates the dissolution of the Western empire and its exploitation by the Germanic tribes, whose free movement within the frontiers was not a new phenomenon, and did not in itself imply the decline of Rome.[88] Undoubtedly, what Christianity as a form of religious life brings is a new logic, what Edward Watts has called that of *Roman Christian progress*, related to God's glorification, which replaces the pagan Roman logic of decline and renewal, related to the glorification of men.[89]

> Paulinus points to the radical but logical conclusion of the story of *Roman Christian progress* that began with Constantine. Its endpoint was not the Christian Roman Empire that fourth-century bishops and emperors imagined. If Roman Christians genuinely thought of themselves as citizens of two worlds, the Civitas of Rome and the Civitas of God, and the Civitas of God was more important, why must the Civitas of Rome still exist? What good did it provide?[90]

The point being made in this quotation is that the community that constituted the 'nation' of the Roman Christian empire driven by that logic, anticipated and seemed to desire the ultimate end or fulfilment of that progress of salvation, which in my terms was the ultimate realisation of the principle of maximising the glory of God through self-sacrifice. A sacrifice of the Roman community — or Civitas of Rome— which, as the writings of Christians of that century testify, came to make reparation for Rome's pagan past.[91] It must be borne in mind that for the Roman Christian community, the real Other was the form of life of imperial Rome, and that while the latter did not succeed in eliminating the Christians, these, nevertheless, with their form of life of glorifying God completed their 'fundamentalist' project of realising an entirely Christian empire by excluding and eliminating their constitutive Other, which was the Roman form of life of maximising freedom and individual goods, or, if you like,

---

world was oppressed by a new species of tyranny; and the persecuted sects became the secret enemies of their country'.

[88] Watts, *The Eternal Decline and Fall of Rome*, p. 100. Answer of Ambrosio to Symmachus.

[89] Watts, *The Eternal Decline and Fall of Rome*, pp. 98: 'confrontation between the traditional Roman model of decline and renewal and this new vision of Rome as a State progressing toward an enlightened Christian future'.

[90] Watts, *The Eternal Decline and Fall of Rome*, p. 116.

[91] Watts, *The Eternal Decline and Fall of Rome*, p. 108.

the glorification of the individual.[92] The *Civitas Dei* wanted to definitively discard the *Roman Civitas*, but as negative constituents, one needs the other. In the middle of the fifth century, Augustine himself argued in his work that for Christians, who were now also Romans, it was not the persistence of the city of men that mattered but the realisation of the city of God: 'Augustine's powerful and innovative rhetoric conveyed his sincere belief that Christians needed to focus on a higher purpose than the health of the Roman civitas'.[93] This logic of progress in the realisation of this 'city of God' was intense in the years after Theodosius, from 380 onwards, having shown a great willingness of 'accelerating progress towards a fully Christian empire'.[94] This change of logic implied a new ethic and a new will-to-be. In this will to win themselves through the Christian Roman progress, they lost their identity and the existence of the —Western— empire, which was divided into kingdoms of Alans, Visigoths, Vandals, Ostrogoths, etc., whose forms of life (Arianism and incipient feudalism) assimilated the properly Roman Christian form. But against what I have just argued, one may wonder why then the Roman Christian form of life was maintained in the eastern empire, in Constantinople,[95] which in the following century became even more Christian and fundamentalist under Emperor Justinian. The answer could be the following:

The barbarian invasions during much of the fifth century were fleeting raids, which ravaged, pillaged and plundered for a limited time but did not generally involve conquest of territory —some settlements were established in agreement with Rome—, and other tribes even collaborated with the Romans to hold off the Huns and to drive the Vandals out of Hispania. This means that Rome maintained its superiority over these tribes both militarily and culturally even during that century, and that their final collapse can be explained as the neglect of earthly power resulting from a surrender of the Roman Christian State to an eschatological destiny of salvation and reparation for the pagan past. In contrast, in the Eastern empire, although there was peace for most of the fifth century,[96] during the following century, incursions came from the barbarians and Slavs as well as from the Persians, especially the latter; for the force of resistance which Byzantium had to apply to defend itself against them resulted in a conflict which lasted for years and remained a stalemate, thanks to which neither could assimilate the other and neither could consolidate and become

---

[92] This will be better understood if read in the light of the humanist and religious forms of life as they appear in my *Forms of life. Some Images of Human Being.* Forthcoming.

[93] *The Eternal Decline and the Fall of Rome*, pp. 112-13.

[94] *The Eternal Decline and the Fall of Rome*, pp. 97-98.

[95] Some, like Theodoric, were more tolerant of the Christian religion, but others, like the Vandals who had settled in North Africa, destroyed churches, humiliated and subjugated priests and bishops and enslaved the population.

[96] Ward-Perkins, *The Fall of Rome and the End of Civilization*, p. 61.

self-founded in their respective forms of life. This changed in the eighth century, when it can be said that the Byzantine Empire came to be cut off from its territories by the dominant force of the Arabs, and the Roman Christian form of life (their Romanness) came to be assimilated by their culture, which exerted its influence from the conquered territories, resulting in a cultural conversion and the restructuring of the civic administrative organisation of Byzantium.[97] In short, if the Western Roman community, while tolerating the settlement of the barbarians on its territory and collaborating with them, is dedicated to integrating itself into their Christian form of life until the final sacrifice, having progressed in the elimination of the form of life of imperial Rome as constitutive Other, on the other hand, the Eastern Roman community, from the end of the fifth century, will see its progress of integration and foundation interrupted by the conflict with the Persians, mutually preventing the totalisation and universalisation of their forms of life with this arduous resistance

Ethics, Generosity and Philosophy

Thus, back to my point, if the ethics of the State implies the obligation of persisting in one's own form of life —whereby the moral imperative and the will-to-be coincide—, the same can be said of the ethics of other non-state communities. The society delimited by the State is the arena of the struggle between different ethics, so that in this struggle, some communities ethically prevent other communities from becoming, or dangerously close to becoming, who they already are. That is, the will to win oneself, which is inherent in every form of life and coincides with its ethics, can only be saved from self-destruction by the opposing will of Others, because it weakens the will of the subject and makes him doubt himself.

Ethics, as that way of behaviour which is good, because it is necessary,[98] driven by the subject's moral will to persist and universalise himself,[99] in a way

---

[97] Heather, *The Fall of the Roman Empire*, p. 431.

[98] 'Ethics' comes from the Greek word *ethos*, which meant precisely a 'way of being and acting' according to Foucault: '[it was] ethical in the sense in which the Greeks unsderstood it: *ethos* was a way of being and of behaviour. It was a mode of being for the subject, along with a certain way of acting, a way visible to others', Michel Foucault, 'The Ethics of the Concern for the Self', in *Foucault Live: Collective Interviews, 1961-1984*, ed. by Sylvere Lotringer (New York: Semiotext(e), 1996), p. 436.

[99] The will is established as morality (being that one is) to which actions refer, and these actions in turn are reinforced by ethical justification. While these actions are ethical in relation to the doctrine of the good, and moral in relation to the will-to-be (they can only be ethical if they respond to morality), they are ideology with respect to the possibilities established as necessary, i.e., with respect to the determination of the form of life as

embraces the problem of the inevitability of the Hobbessian struggle between different communities and the rise of one as hegemonic over others. In fact, in the absence of the spontaneous generosity of the subject who opens himself to the being of Others temporarily and inexplicably, rocked in the nothingness of life and silence, it is the ethics of Others that saves us from our own ethics — our own ethics can, in fact, destroy us. And the same can be said about the State with respect to other States; when there is no generosity, it is the ethics of other States that has to save the State from its own self-destruction. The Hobbesian struggle of all against all as a *state of nature* is thus subsumed in the *political State* in which particular freedoms are constituted against the background of all those freedoms that are not contemplated and are rather cancelled and superseded. In such a political State it is opposition and resistance that maintain both the persistence of being and one's own identity. All hegemony implies assimilation, and assimilation is the negation of the Other, which is why we have moved from the sword of the Hobbesian monarch to the individual self-imposition of habits through identification and to propaganda for the strengthening of the will. Imposition for its own sake, i.e., the sword, does not make a form of life hegemonic, but the assimilation of other communities through the weakening of the will-to-be that differentiates them. This homogenisation, as has been shown, is the State to which the struggle tends after a temporary balance of forces in resistance. And after the ephemeral time of struggle, what follows is the hegemony of one side and a no less ephemeral peace.

The reason for the above is that the peace of hegemony is illusory, and hence its inherent problem: that of an ethical discourse that justifies a behaviour born of the will-to-be-and-to-power, and, therefore, not born of the purported universal reason. In a word, it is an ethical discourse that justifies the unjustifiable before a universal audience. The only way to overcome such an ethics is through generosity. And not an 'ethics of generosity', which is antithetical. For one cannot prescribe 'losing oneself in order to gain oneself'. Otherwise, losing oneself would be the result of the will, which would give rise to an *ethics of renunciation*. But generosity is not the self-imposed obligation of renunciation but the absence of will, its spontaneous suspension. In the will to renounce, there is a paradoxical will to cancel the will, which leads only to an ethics in contradiction with itself. But if one cannot prescribe 'losing oneself in order to gain oneself' —gaining oneself as an openness to the multiple constitutive possibilities of being—, neither can one prohibit 'gaining oneself, which leads to the loss of oneself' —loss as the possibility of continuing to be—, for this would be to prohibit the will-to-be, since 'to gain oneself' is to

---

possibility. In a word, ideology is necessary behaviour and ethics is the same behaviour from its justification as good behaviour for the subject and his community.

progressively realise oneself in this real being that one already is in potentiality. Generosity is not necessary and, therefore, cannot be given either as a prescription or as a prohibition, and therefore, it cannot be an ethics.

Generosity can be grasped as the understanding of the uselessness of the will-to-be —the 'useless passion' or *passion inutile*[100] referred to by Sartre— and the revelation of the deception of universal and hegemonic ethics as a created necessity. This leads to the momentary spontaneous cessation of the will-to-be, thus also suspending one's own being and allowing Others to be. Thus contemplated, generosity is a cherished moment of basking in the possibilities of the will before its determination, in the will-to-will of all beings, in the kaleidoscopic experience of every being... But from this generosity, can we understand the Other as a particular determination of the will-to-be? If we could understand the Other in the law or principle that governs him, we would be determining ourselves according to that law or principle, because understanding is sharing that principle; understanding is wanting to act and be in that particular way.[101] Otherwise, we are not talking about understanding, but about assuming or projecting our own principles, values and categories onto the other, i.e., assimilating, which is the most common. To project and assume is not to understand. As has been said from the beginning of this book, understanding is the spontaneity of meaning, and meaning arises from the form of life we realise; the opposite becomes absurd. That is why generosity cannot lead us to understand the Other, for then we would be sharing their principle and will-to-be, so that the Other would no longer be such. However, the essence of the generous act is that we allow the Other to be Other, without understanding him and without wanting to assimilate him: we allow him to be as the Other wants to be and realise himself in the world. Generosity enables us to open ourselves to the possibility of other beings, and therefore other forms of life, without this plurality meaning that we understand or adhere to any of them, for if this were to happen, our generosity would end at the same time. To understand, to adhere, to identify, etc., is to share an interest, whereas generosity is essentially disinterested.

According to the above, this generosity can never be the basis of an ethics of generosity, but only an attitude of indeterminacy and freedom. It is with this attitude that every community and every State is challenged in its legitimacy. This attitude, as has been shown, arises from the non-causal and, therefore, non-explainable understanding of the absurdity of being insofar as there is no other option than to be what one is not, for one can only be when a contingent

---

[100] Jean-Paul Sartre, *L'être et le néant* (Paris: Gallimard, 1943), p. 662. In *Being and Nothingness* (New York: Philosohical Library, 1956), p. 615.
[101] See Jean-Paul Sartre, *Critique of Dialectical Reason*, I, p. 509.

possibility becomes necessary and ethically justified. In this sense, philosophy, as a form of life, is naturally always on the threshold of generosity, because it keeps the philosopher —the one that has not been assimilated— on the threshold of the doubt of being with the consequent weakness of the will. The philosopher's being is to question his own being when he understands that he is driven necessarily to be that which he is not. In such an understanding, the abyss of generosity is glimpsed. *Philosophy, doubt* —with the weakening of the will— and *generosity* are the essential enemies of all politics and of every nation State that has failed in its assimilation strategy, and for the same reason, they are the greatest antidote (*Pharmakon*) against the elimination of the Other and consequent self-destruction. For philosophy, insofar as it questions the necessity of the imposed being —even that of its own being—, is a *sub-versive* form of life: it seeks to show that beneath what is imposed as necessary, other possibilities are hidden; this is *subversion*, i.e., showing other versions that lie beneath the imposed one. Now, if philosophy as a trigger for generosity leads to doubt and doubt leads to letting Others be, or in any case to a possible conversion, that is, *ceasing to be what one was in order to be something else*, on the contrary, the self-foundation of one resulting from the elimination of the constitutive Other leads to *an absolute ceasing to be and to exist*. Thus, *persisting in being* is a delicate balance between conversion —assimilated by the Other— and self-destruction —through assimilation and/or expulsion of the Other.

Bibliography

Al-Saji, Alia, 'The racialization of Muslim Veils: A Philosophical Analysis', in *Philosophy and Social Criticism*, 36:8 (2010) https://doi.org/10.1177/019145 3710375589.

Anantharaman, Muralikumar, 'China Bars Foreign Curricula, Ownership in Some Private Schools', *Reuters*, 17 May 2021 https://www.reuters.com /world/china/china-bars-foreign-curriculum-ownership-some-private-school s -2021-05-17/, [accessed 30 October 2023].

Apel, Karl-Otto, *From a Transcendental-Semiotic Point of View* (Manchester and New York: Manchester University Press, 1998).

Aristotle, *Complete Works*, edited by Jonathan Barnes (Princeton, Jersey: Princeton University Press, 1995).

Austin, John, *How to do Things with Words* (Cambridge: Harvad University Press, 1962).

Badiou, Alain, *Being and Event* (London: Continuum, 2006).

Badiou, Alain, *Can Politics be Thought?* (Durham and London: Duke University Press, 2018).

Bhopal, Kalwant and Martin Myers, *Insiders, Outsiders and Others. Gypsies and Identity* (Hatfield, Hertfordshire: University of Hertfordshire Press, 2008).

Boas, Franz, *Anthropology and Modern Life* (New York: Norton & Company, 1962).

Bourdieu, Pierre, *The Logic of Practice* (Stanford, California: Stanford University Press, 1990).

Breazeale, Daniel, 'How to Make an Existentialist?' in *Fichte and the Phenomenological Tradition*, ed. by Violetta Waibel, Daniel Breazeale, Tom Rockmore (Berlin: De Gruyter, 2010).

Brown, Kerry, *China's World. What Does China Want?* (London and New York: I. B. Tauris, 2017).

Bunker, Jenny, 'Ethics and Will in Schopenhauer's Philosophy', in *The Concept of Will in Classical German Philosophy*, ed. by Manja Kisner and Jörg Noller (Berlin and Boston: De Gruyter, 2020).

Butler, Judith, 'Competing Universalities', in Judith Butler, Ernesto Laclau y Slavoj Žižek, *Contingency, Hegemony, and Universality* (London and New York: Verso, 2000).

Butler, Judith, *The Psychic Life of Power* (California, Stanford: Stanford University Press, 1997).

CGTN, 'China Bans Tutoring Institutions in Core Schools Subjects From IPO', 24 July 2021, https://news.cgtn.com/news/2021-07-24/China-issues-docume nt-to-regulate-after-school-tutoring-12a4svQVeH6/index.html [accessed 30 October 2023].

Caiyu, Liu, 'Chinese Lawmaker Proposes Removing English as Core Subject', *Global Times*, 5 March 2021, https://www.globaltimes.cn/page/202103/12 17396.shtml, [accessed 29 October 2023].

Chomsky, Noam, 'Notes on Anarchism', in *Chomsky on Anarchism*, selected and edited by Barry Pateman (Edinburgh, Oakland, West Virginia: AK Press, 2005).

Chomsky, Noam, 'Containing the Threat of Democracy', in *Chomsky on Anarchism*, selected and edited by Barry Pateman (Edinburgh, Oakland, West Virginia: AK Press, 2005).

Ci, Jiwei, *Democracy in China. The Coming Crisis* (London and Massachusetts: Havard University Press, 2019).

Claessen, Henri and Peter Skalník, 'The Early State: Models and Reality', in *The Early State*, ed. by Claessen and Skalník (The Hague, The Netherlands: Mouton, 1978).

Collingwood, Robin George, *The New Leviathan. Or Man, Society, Civilization and Barbarism* (Oxford: Clarendon Press, 1942).

Cornette, Joël, *La Mort de Louis XIV: Apogée et crépuscule de la royauté* (Paris: Gallimard, 2015).

Csepregi, Botond, 'Gypsies in Europe', interview to Szilveszter Póczik, published originally in Hungarian in *Confessio*, 4 (2010). Translated by *Reformed Church in Hungary*, https://reformatus.hu/english/news/gypsies-in-europe_poczik/ [accessed 29 October 2023].

Dahl, Robert A., 'The Concept of Power', *Behavioural Science*, 2 (1957).

Dalrymple, Theodore, 'The European Way of Life', *Law and Liberty*, 24 September 2019, https:/lawliberty.org/the-european-way-of-life/ [accessed 30 October 2023].

D'Amato, David S, 'Understanding the Modern State', *Libertarianism* https://www.libertarianism.org/columns/understanding-modern-state [accessed 28 October 2023].

Darwin, Charles, *The Origin of Species by Means of Natural Selection* (Cambridge: Cambridge University Press, 2009).

Deleuze, Gilles, *Pure Immanence. Essays on a Life* (New York: Zone Books, 2001).

Enarssona, Therese and Simon Lindgrenb, 'Free speech or hate speech? A legal analysis of the discourse about Roma on Twitter', *Information and Communications Technology Law*, 28 (2018), https://doi.org/10.1080 /1360 0834.2018.1494415.

European Commission, 'Promoting our Way of Life', https://commission.euro pa.eu/strategy-and-policy/priorities-2019-2024/promoting-our-european-wa y-life_en [accessed 29 October 2023].

Farr, Arnold L., 'The Other and the Necessary Conditions of the Self in Fichte's *Wissenschaftslehre* and Paul Ricoeur's Phenomenology of the Will', in *Fichte and the Phenomenological Tradition*, ed. by Violetta Waibel, Daniel Breazeale, Tom Rockmore (Berlin: De Gruyter, 2010).

Fichte, Johann Gottlieb, *System of Ethics. According to the Principles of the Wissenschaftslehre*, ed. by Daniel Breazeale (Cambridge: Cambridge University Press, 2005).

Fichte, Johann Gottlieb, *Foundations of the Transcendental Philosophy. Wissenschaftlehre Nova Methodo (1796/1799)*, ed. and trans. by Daniel Breazeale (Ithaca and London: Cornell University Press, 1992).

Fichte, Johann Gottlieb, *Foundations of Natural Right* (Cambridge: Cambridge University Press, 2000).

Fichte, Johann Gottlieb, *The Science of Knowledge* (London: Trübner & Co. Ludgate Hill, 1889).

Fichte, Johann Gottlieb, *The Science of Knowing. J. G Fichte's 1804 Lectures on the Wissenschaftslehre* (Albany: State University of New York Press, 2005).

Fichte, Johann Gottlieb, *Addresses to the German Nation* (Cambridge: Cambridge University Press, 2009).

Fichte, Johann Gottlieb, 'The Characteristics of the Present Age', in *Popular Works*, 2 vols (London: Trübner & Co, Ludgate Hill, 1889).

Fichte, Johann Gottlieb, *Die Grundzüge des gengenwartigen Zeltalters* (Leipzig: Verlag von Felix Meiner, 1908).

Foucault, Michel, 'The Subject and Power', translated by Leslie Sawyer, *Critical Inquiry*, 8:4 (1982).

Foucault, Michel, 'The Ethics of the Concern for the Self', in *Foucault Live: Collective Interviews, 1961-1984*, ed. by Sylvere Lotringer (New York: Semiotext(e), 1996).

Foucault, Michel, *Society Must Be Defended. Lectures at the Collège de France 1975-1976* (New York: Picador, 2003).

Foucault, Michel, *Security, Territory and Population. Lectures at the Collège de France 1977-78* (New York: Palgrave Macmillan, 2009).

Frankfurt, Harry, 'Freedom of the Will and the Concept of a Person', *The Journal of Philosophy*, 68 (1971).

Fukuyama, Francis, *The End of History and the Last Man* (New York: The Free Press, 1992).

Gibbon, Edward, *The Decline and Fall of the Roman Empire*, volume 4, ed. by J. B. Bury (London: Methuen & Co., 1897).

Graeber, David, *Bullshit Jobs* (New York: Simon & Schuster, 2018).

Graeber, David and David Wengrow, *The Dawn of Everything. A New History of Humanity* (London, UK: Allen Lane, Penguin Books Limited, 2021).

Graeber, David and Marshall Sahlins, *On Kings* (Chicago: Hau Books, 2017).

Gray, John, *Liberalism* (Minneapolis: University of Minnesota Press, 2003).

Han, Byung-Chul, *The Expulsion of the Other. Society, Perception and Communication Today* (Cambridge: Polity Press, 2018).

Han, Byung-Chul, *What is Power?* (Cambridge: Polity Press, 2019).

Han, Byung-Chul, *The Disappearance of Rituals* (Cambridge: Polity Press, 2020).

Hancourt, Bernard, *Exposed: Desire and Disobedience in the Digital Age* (Cambridge: Harvard University Press, 2015).

Hartmann, Nicolai, *New ways of Ontology* (Chicago: Henry Regnery Company, 1953).

Heaslip, Vanessa, Denise Wilson and Debra Jackson, 'Are Gypsy Roma Traveller communities indigenous and would identification as such better address their public health needs?' *Public Health*, 176 (2019), https://doi.org/10.1016/j.puhe.2019.02.020.

Heather, Peter, *The Fall of the Roman Empire. A New History of Rome and the Barbarians* (New York: Oxford University Press, 2006).

Hegel, Georg Wilhelm Friedrich, *Elements of the Philosophy of Right* (Cambridge: Cambridge University Press, 2003).

Heidegger, Martin, *Being and Time* (London: Blackwell, 1927/2001).

Heidegger, Martin, *Nietzsche: The Will to Power as Art*, 2 vols (San Francisco: Harper, 1991).

Hufendiek, Rebekka, *Embodied Emotions* (London and New York: Routledge, 2016).

Husserl, Edmund, *The Crisis of European Sciences and Transcendental Phenomenology* (Evanston, Illinois: Northwestern University Press, 1970).

Husserl, Edmund, *Ideas Pertaining to a Pure Phenomenology and to a Phenomenological Philosophy, First Book: General Introduction*, volume 2 of *Collected Works* (Dordrecht, The Netherlands: Kluwer Academic Publishers, 1983).

Jachtenfuchs, Markus, 'The monopoly of legitimate force: denationalization, or business as usual?' In *The Transformation of the State*, ed. by Stephan Leibfried and Michael Zurn (Cambridge: Cambridge University Press, 2005).

Kant, Immanuel, *Critique of Pure Reason*, translated and edited by Paul Guyer and Allen Wood (New York: Cambridge University Press, 2000).

Kishik, David, *Wittgenstein's Form of Life* (London: Continuum, 2008).

Kisner, Manja, 'Drive and Will in Fichte's *System of Ethics*', in *The Concept of Will in Classical German Philosophy*, ed. by Manja Kisner and Jörg Noller (Berlin and Boston: De Gruyter, 2020).

Kofman, Sarah, *Nietzsche et la Métaphore* (Paris: Galilée, 1983).

Koshakoba, Natalia B., 'Yoruba City-State', in *The Early State*, ed. by Claessen and Skalník (The Hague, The Netherlands: Mouton, 1978).

Krause, Karl Christian Friedrich, *Das Urbild des Menscheit* (Göttingen: Dieterichschen Buchhandlung, 1851).

Krause, Karl Christian Friedrich, *The Ideal of Humanity and the Universal Federation*, edited by W. Hastie (Edinburgh: T&T Clark, 1900).

Laclau, Ernesto, 'Identity and Hegemony: The Role of Universality in the Constitution of Political Logics', in Judith Butler, Ernesto Laclau y Slavoj Žižek, *Contingency, Hegemony, and Universality* (London and New York: Verso, 2000).

Laclau, Ernesto, *On Populist Reason* (London and New York: Verso, 2005).

Laertius, Diogenes, *Lives of the Eminent Philosophers*, trans. by Pamela Mensch and ed. by James Miller (New York: Oxford University Press, 2018).

Levinas, Emmanuel, *Totality and Infinity: An Essay on Exteriority* (London, Boston, The Hague: Martinus Nijhoff Publishers, 1979).

Lewellen, Ted, *Political Anthropology: An Introduction*, Foreword by Victor Turner (Westport, Connecticut: Praeger, 2003).

Lorenzini, Daniele, 'From Counter-Conduct to Critical Attitude: Michel Foucault and the Art of Not Being Governed Quite So Much', in *Foucault Studies*, 21 (2016).

Love, John R., *Antiquity and Capitalism* (London and New York: Routledge, 2005).

Martínez Guillem, Susana, 'European Identity: Across Which Lines? Defining Europe Through Public Discourses on the Roma', *Journal of International and Intercultural Communication*, 4:1 (2011).

McGuigan, Jim, 'The Neoliberal Self'. *Culture Unbound*, 6:1 (2014).

Miller, David, *Strangers in our Midst. The political Philosophy of Immigration* (Cambridge, Massachusetts: Harvard University Press, 2016).

Nancy, Jean-Luc, 'The Image: mimesis and methexis', *Nancy and Visual Culture*, ed. by Adrienne Janus and Carrie Giunta (Edinburgh: Edinburgh University Press, 2016).

Ngo, Helen, *Habits of Racism: A Phenomenology of Racism and Racialized embodiment* (London and New York: Lexington Book, 2017).

Nietzsche, Friedrich, *The Will to Power* (New York: Vintage Books, Random House, 1968).

Nietzsche, Friedrich, *Thus Spoke Zarathustra* (Cambridge: Cambridge University Press, 2005).

Noller, Jörg, '"Will is Primal Being": Schelling Critical Voluntarism', in *The Concept of Will in German Idealism* (Berlin: De Gruyter, 2020).

Pew Research Center, 'EU View of Roma, Muslim, Jews', In *A Fragile Rebound for EU Image on Eve of European Parliament Elections*. Report 12 May 2014, https://www.pewresearch.org/global/2014/05/12/chapter-4-views-of-roma -muslims-jews/ [accessed 29 October 2023].

Rametta, Gaetano, 'Consciousness. A Comparison between Fichte and the Young Sartre', in Fichte and the Phenomenological Tradition, ed. by Violetta Waibel, Daniel Breazeale and Tom Rockmore (Berlin: De Gruyter, 2010).

Rettman, Andrew, 'France Pushes "European Way of Life" Amid Macron Re-election Bid', *Euobserver*, 8 February 2022, https://euobserver.com/rule-of-law/154306 [accessed 29 October 2023].

Ricoeur, Paul, *Freedom and Nature: The Voluntary and the Involuntary* (Evanston, Illinois: Northwestern University Press, 1966).

Ricoeur, Paul, *Oneself as Another* (Chicago and London: The University of Chicago Press, 1992).

Ricoeur, Paul, *The Course of Recognition* (Cambridge, Massachusetts: Harvard University Press, 2005).

Robinson, Garrett, 'The Common Good Before the Modern State', *The Regensburg Forum*, https://regensburgforum.com/2019/09/02/the-common-good-before-the-modernstate/#_ft n1 [accessed 28 October 2023].

Roman, Christopher, 'The Counter-Conduct of Medieval Hermits', *Foucault Studies*, 21 (2017).

Rosenblum, Cassady, 'Work is a False Idol', in *The New York Times*, 22 August 2021.

Rueda Garrido, Daniel, *Forms of Life and Subjectivity: Rethinking Sartre's Philosophy* (Cambridge: Open Books Publishers, 2021).

Rueda Garrido, Daniel, 'Imitation, Conscious Will and Social Conditioning', *Mind and Society*, 20 (2021).

Rueda Garrido, Daniel, 'Forms of Life and The Phenomenological Ontology of Conversion,' *Sophia. International Journal of Philosophy and Traditions*, 62 (2023), https://doi.org/10.1007/s11841-021-00838-4.

Rueda Garrido, Daniel, *Forms of Life: Propaganda and Ideology* (Cambridge: Ethics Press, 2023).

Ryder, Andrew Richard, Iulius Rostas & Marius Taba, '"Nothing about us without us": the role of inclusive community development in school desegregation for

Roma communities', *Race Ethnicity and Education*, 17:4 (2014), http://dx.doi .org/10.1080/136133 24.2014.885426.

Sarris, Peter, *Empires of Faith* (New York: Oxford University Press, 2011).

Sartre, Jean-Paul, *Being and Nothingness* (New York: Philosophical Library, 1956).

Sartre, Jean-Paul, *L'être et le néant* (Paris: Gallimard, 1943).

Sartre, Jean-Paul, *The Imaginary. A Phenomenological Psychology of the Imagination* (London and New York: Routledge, 2004).

Sartre, Jean-Paul, *Existentialism and Humanism* (London: Methuen, 1946).

Sartre, Jean-Paul, *Critique of Dialectical Reason*, Volume 1 (London and New York: Verso, 2004).

Sartre, Jean-Paul, *L'existentialisme est un humanisme* (Paris: Les Éditions Nagel, 1966).

Schaedel, Richard P., 'Early State of the Incas', in *The Early State*, ed. by Claessen and Skalník (The Hague, The Netherlands: Mouton, 1978).

Scheff, Thomas J., *Emotions, the Social Bond and Human Reality. Part/Whole Analysis* (New York: Cambridge University Press, 1997).

Scheler, Max, *Die Stellung des Menschen in Kosmos* (Bonn: Bouvier Verlag, 1991).

Schelling, Wilhelm Joseph, *Philosophical Investigations into the Essence of Human Freedom* (New York, Albany: State University of New York, 2006).

Schopenhauer, Arthur, *The World as Will and Representation*, 2 vols (New York: Dover Publications, Inc., 1969).

Sedov, Leonid A., 'Angkor: Society and State', in *The Early State*, ed. by Claessen and Skalník (The Hague, The Netherlands: Mouton, 1978).

Sen, Amartya, *Identity and Violence* (New York and London: Norton and Company, 2007).

Shahar, Shulamith, 'Religious Minorities, Vagabonds and Gypsies in Early Modern Europe', in *The Roma. A Minority in Europe. Historical, Political and Social Perspectives*, ed. by Roni Stauber and Raphael Vago (Budapest and New York: Central European University Press, 2007).

Shuo, Zou, 'Debate Rages Over Proposal to Ax English', *China Daily*, 8 March 2021, https://www.chinadaily.com.cn/a/202103/08/WS60457153a31024ad0 aad756.html [accessed 29 October 2023].

Sloterdijk, Peter, *Critique of Cynical Reason* (Minneapolis and London: University of Minnesota Press, 2001).

Spinoza, Benedictus, *Complete Works* (Indianapolis, Cambridge: Hackett Publishing Company, 2002).

Strayer, Joseph R., *On the Medieval Origins of the Modern State* (Princeton: Princepton University Press, 1970).

Susskind, Richard and Susskind, Daniel, *The Future of Professions. How Technology Will Transform the Work of Human Experts* (Oxford: Oxford University Press, 2015).

Szanto, Thomas, 'The Phenomenology of Shared Emotions. Reassessing Gerda Walther', in *Women Phenomenologists on Social Ontology*, ed. by S. Luft and R. Hagengruber (Switzerland: Springer Nature, 2018).

Taylor, Charles, *Modern Social Imaginaries* (Durham and London: Duke University Press, 2004).

The Bible, English Standard Version (ESV) and New King James Version (NKJV). *Bible Hub* https://biblehub.com/ [accessed 28 October 2023].

'The low-desire life: why people in China are rejecting high-pressure jobs in favour of "lying flat", *The Guardian*, 5 July 2021, https://www.theguardian .com/world/2021/jul/05/the-low-desire-life-why-people-in-china-are-rejec ting-high-pressure-jobs-in-favour-of-lying flat [accessed 28 October 2023].

Tilly, Charles, *Coercion, Capital and European State AD 990-1990* (Oxford: Basil Blackwell, 1990).

'Ukraine war: Russia's 'propaganda warriors' pushing for use of nuclear weapons, Nobel laureate warns', *South China Morning Post*, 4 May 2022 http s://www.scmp.com/news/world/russia-central-asia/article/3176425/ukrain e-war-russias-propaganda-warriors-arearguing?campaign=3176425&modul e =perpetual_scroll_0&p gtype=article [accessed 29 October 2023].

Volkan, Vamik D., *Immigrants and Refugees. Trauma, Perennial Mourning, Prejudice, and Border Psychology* (London: Karnac Books, 2017).

Ward-Perkins, Bryan, *The Fall of Rome and the End of Civilization* (New York: Oxford University Press, 2005).

Watts, Edward J., *The Eternal Decline and Fall of Rome* (New York: Oxford University Press, 2021).

Weber, Max, *Economy and Society*, volume 2 (New York: Bedminster, 1968).

Weber, Max, *The Agrarian Sociology of Ancient Civilizations* (London, New Left Books, 1976).

Weber, Max, *The Protestant Ethics and the Spirit of Capitalism* (London and New York: Routledge, 2005).

'What is XR?' *Extinction Rebellion* https://rebellion.global/ [accessed 28 October 2023].

Wittgenstein, Ludwig, *Tractatus Logico-Philosophicus* (London: Routledge and Kegan Paul Ltd, 1961).

Wittgenstein, Ludwig, *Philosophical Investigations* (Oxford: Blackwell, 1958).

Whorf, Benjamin Lee, *Language, Thought and Reality* (Cambridge, Massachusetts: the MIT Press, 1978).

Wolf, Eric, *Pathways of Power. Building an Anthropology of the Wodern World* (London, Berkely and Los Angeles: University of California Press, 2001).

Yan, Alice, 'Hongkongers living in mainland China say safety and friendships are on the line amid protests', *South Cina Morning Post*, 16 December 2019 https://www.scmp.com/news/china/society/article/3041417/hongkongers-living-mainland-china-say-safety-and-friendships-are?module=perpetual_s croll_0&pgtype=article&campa ign=3041417 [accessed 29 October 2023].

Zahavi, Dan, 'We in Me or Me in We? Collective Intentionality and Selfhood', *Journal of Social Ontology*, Published Online First (2021).

Zahavi, Dan, 'Empathy and Mirroring: Husserl and Gallese', in *Life, Subjectivity & Art: Essays in Honor of Rudolf Bernet*, ed. by Roland Breeur and Ullrich Melle (Dordrecht: Springer, 2012).

Zambrano, María, *Filosofía y poesía* (México D. F.: Fondo de Cultura Económica, 2005).

Zambrano, María, *Notas para un método* (Madrid: Mondadori, 1989).

Zambrano, María, *El sueño creador* (Zamora, Veracruz: Universidad Veracruzana, 1965).

Žižek, Slavoj, *The Sublime Object of Ideology* (London and New York: Verso, 1989).

Žižek, Slavoj, *Enjoy Your Symptom!* (London and New York: Routledge, 1992).

Žižek, Slavoj, 'Class Struggle or Postmodernism? Yes, please!', in Judith Butler, Ernesto Laclau and Slavoj Žižek, *Contingency, Hegemony, and Universality* (London and New York: Verso, 2000).

Index

www.ingramcontent.com/pod-product-compliance
Lightning Source LLC
Chambersburg PA
CBHW062039270326
41929CB00014B/2479